# ROLAND ALLEN'S
# THE MINISTRY OF EXPANSION

Roland Allen saw clearly in the first half of the twentieth century what few over the last two millennia have seen and even today see: that there is an essential interrelationship between the charismatic working of the Holy Spirit, the dynamic nature of the church as the body of Christ and the fellowship of the Spirit, and the mission of the triune God. Although here applied to the very specific question of sacramental and eucharistic practice, the implications and applications of Allen's vision are extensive for all committed to participating in the work of the Spirit to and from the ends of the earth. While always respecting the role of the institutional dimensions of the church, Allen here prompts us to wrestle again and again with apostolic life in the Spirit as normative for engaging the ongoing missio Dei, however difficult such may be to discern at times.

Amos Yong, PhD
professor of theology and mission
Fuller Seminary
author of *The Missiological Spirit* (2014) and *Spirit of Love* (2012)

WCL, J.D. Payne, and the contributors are to be congratulated on the release of this previously unpublished work by Roland Allen. We hear much today about the importance of empowering and mobilizing ordinary Christians for the cause of multiplying and growing healthy churches. This little book demonstrates how Roland Allen on this important principle—particularly as it relates to celebration of the Lord's Supper—was once again ahead of his time. Readers familiar with Allen's biblically reasoned challenges to unhelpful traditions will not be disappointed by this work.

Craig Ott, PhD
professor of mission and intercultural studies
Trinity Evangelical Divinity School

I still remember first encountering Roland Allen's writings as a student. His prose was lively. His insights were relevant. His thoughts were imbued with Scripture. Since Allen died in 1947, surely everything of significance the man wrote has been published by now. But no! New treasures await you. J. D. Payne has done us a great service by bringing to light a previously unpublished manuscript by Allen. Readers of Allen will feel that they are sitting down with an old friend to revisit some common themes from slightly different angles (and new anecdotes). Payne himself has written a helpful introductory chapter and lined up other scholars (Hubert Allen, Robert Schmidt, Steven Rutt, Robert Banks) to provide essays related to Roland Allen's thought or life. What a treasure this little book is!

ROBERT L. PLUMMER, PHD
chairman of New Testament department
professor of New Testament interpretation
The Southern Baptist Theological Seminary

Sixty years ago Donald McGavran reintroduced Roland Allen to evangelicals. McGavran often spoke and wrote about how much Roland Allen had influenced his own missiology. McGavran required his students to read Allen's books and revived interest in Allen's approach to missions strategy. J. D. Payne and his collaborators have performed a similar service for a new generation of evangelicals. In this volume they have provided missiologists, missionaries, and missions students with a long unpublished Allen manuscript. The manuscript revisits common themes in Allen's writings: the role of the Holy Spirit in missions, the spontaneous growth of new churches, and the importance of lay ministry. The essays by Allen scholars enhance the value of the book, and the chapter by Hubert Allen, Roland's grandson, is most welcome.

JOHN MARK TERRY, PHD
professor of missions
Mid-America Baptist Theological Seminary

ROLAND ALLEN'S

# THE MINISTRY OF EXPANSION
## THE PRIESTHOOD OF THE LAITY

J.D. PAYNE
EDITOR

**WILLIAM CAREY**
LIBRARY

*Roland Allen's The Ministry of Expansion: The Priesthood of the Laity*
Copyright © 2017 by Hubert Allen
All rights reserved.

No part of this book may be reproduced, stored in a retrieval system, or transmitted in any form or by any means—electronic, mechanical, photocopy, recording, or otherwise—without prior written permission of the publisher, except brief quotations used in connection with reviews in magazines or newspapers. For permission, email permissions@wclboks.com.

Scripture quotations marked (ASV) are from the American Standard Version. Public domain.

Scripture quotations marked (KJV) are from The Authorized (King James) Version. Rights in the Authorized Version in the United Kingdom are vested in the Crown. Reproduced by permission of the Crown's patentee, Cambridge University Press.

Scripture quotations marked (WEB) are from Webster's Bible Translation. Public domain.

Published by William Carey Library, an imprint of William Carey Publishing
10 W. Dry Creek Circle
Littleton, CO 80120 | www.missionbooks.org

Melissa Hughes, editor
Joanne Liang, graphic design

William Carey Library is a ministry of Frontier Ventures
Pasadena, CA 91104 | www.frontierventures.org

23 22 21 20 19 Printed for Worldwide Distribution

---

Library of Congress Cataloging-in-Publication Data

Names: Allen, Roland, 1869-1947, author. | Payne, Jervis David, 1974- editor.
Title: Roland Allen's the ministry of expansion : the priesthood of the laity / J.D. Payne, editor.
Other titles: Ministry of expansion
Description: Pasadena, CA : William Carey Library, 2017. | Includes
   bibliographical references. |
Identifiers: LCCN 2017015722 (print) | LCCN 2017018826 (ebook) | ISBN 9780878086764 (eBook) | ISBN 9780878083008 (pbk.) | ISBN 0878083006 (pbk.)
Subjects: LCSH: Laity. | Lay ministry. | Clergy--Supply and demand. | Church growth. | Missions--Theory. | Allen, Roland, 1869-1947. Ministry of expansion.
Classification: LCC BV687 (ebook) | LCC BV687 .A45 2017 (print) | DDC 266--dc23
LC record available at https://lccn.loc.gov/2017015722

*To Him Who is able to bring about the spontaneous expansion of the Church*

OTHER BOOKS BY J. D. PAYNE

*Missional House Churches*
*The Barnabas Factors*
*Discovering Church Planting*
*Evangelism*
*Roland Allen*
*Kingdom Expressions*
*Strangers Next Door*
*Pressure Points*
*Developing a Strategy for Missions* (co-author)
*Missionary Methods* (co-edited)
*To the Edge*
*Apostolic Church Planting*

# CONTENTS

CONTRIBUTORS . . . . . . . . . . . . . . . . . . . . . . . . . . . . . . . . . . . . . . . . . XIII

ACKNOWLEDGMENTS . . . . . . . . . . . . . . . . . . . . . . . . . . . . . . . . . . . XVII

## PART I
## Background

ROLAND ALLEN: MISSIOLOGY AND *THE MINISTRY OF EXPANSION* . . . . . . . . 3
    J. D. Payne

ROLAND ALLEN: A BIOGRAPHICAL NOTE . . . . . . . . . . . . . . . . . . . . . . . . 19
    Hubert Allen

*THE MINISTRY OF EXPANSION* AND CONTEMPORARY CRISES . . . . . . . . . . . 31
    Robert Schmidt

BACKGROUND AND OVERVIEW OF *THE MINISTRY OF EXPANSION* . . . . . . . . 47
    Steven Rutt

## PART II
## Roland Allen's *The Ministry of Expansion:*
## *The Priesthood of the Laity*

PREFACE . . . . . . . . . . . . . . . . . . . . . . . . . . . . . . . . . . . . . . . . . . . . . . 71

1 | THE FUNDAMENTAL PRINCIPLES . . . . . . . . . . . . . . . . . . . . . . . . . . . 75

2 | HABIT AND TRADITION . . . . . . . . . . . . . . . . . . . . . . . . . . . . . . . . . 83

3 | CHARISMATIC MINISTRY . . . . . . . . . . . . . . . . . . . . . . . . . . . . . . . . . . . 91
4 | THE PRACTICE OF THE EARLY CHURCH. . . . . . . . . . . . . . . . . . . . . . . 101
5 | WE CANNOT GO BACK . . . . . . . . . . . . . . . . . . . . . . . . . . . . . . . . . . . .111
6 | THE PRIESTHOOD OF THE LAITY . . . . . . . . . . . . . . . . . . . . . . . . . . . .121
7 | PRESUMPTION. . . . . . . . . . . . . . . . . . . . . . . . . . . . . . . . . . . . . . . . . 133

POSTSCRIPT. . . . . . . . . . . . . . . . . . . . . . . . . . . . . . . . . . . . . . . . . . . . . . . 147
  *THE FAMILY RITE:* AN INTRODUCTION
  *Robert Banks*

BIBLIOGRAPHY. . . . . . . . . . . . . . . . . . . . . . . . . . . . . . . . . . . . . . . . . . . . .151

# CONTRIBUTORS

**Hubert Allen (MA, University of Oxford; MSocSci, University of Birmingham)** is the grandson of Roland Allen and author of *Roland Allen: Pioneer, Priest, and Prophet*. He was raised in East Africa and later graduated from Oxford. He worked for several years in Uganda, and subsequently taught public administration in Northern Nigeria and in the Dominican Republic, before becoming the Director of Training for IULA (the International Union of Local Authorities), based in The Hague. Subsequently he returned to live in Oxford, working as an independent consultant with Birmingham University's Institute of Local Government Studies, and with various Danish, Dutch, German, and international agencies. Since final retirement and the loss of his beloved Irish wife after prolonged dementia, he has been continuously active, both for his local Anglican Church and ecumenically. He continues to make himself useful as a "healthy control" for medical research, and by applauding the success of his three gifted children and six grandchildren.

**Roland Allen (1868–1947)** served as an Anglican deacon and priest in England, as a missionary to China during the late nineteenth and early twentieth centuries, and also served the church in Kenya. He was the author of numerous articles and books, including: *Missionary Methods: St. Paul's or Ours?*, *The Spontaneous Expansion of the Church and the Causes which Hinder It*, *Missionary Principles*, *Pentecost and the World*, and *The Case for Voluntary Clergy*. He was one of the most influential mission thinkers of the twentieth century.

**Robert Banks (PhD, University of Cambridge)** is a theologian and practitioner who was formerly professor of the ministry of the laity and director of the De Pree Leadership Centre at Fuller Theological Seminary in Los Angeles. He is currently an honorary professor at Alphacrucis College in Sydney and adjunct professor at the Biblical Graduate School of Theology in Singapore. He has written several award-winning books on biblical, theological, ethical, and practical issues. These include books on early Christian as well as contemporary forms of house church life and mission.

**J. D. Payne (PhD, Southern Baptist Theological Seminary)** is the pastor of church multiplication with The Church at Brook Hills in Birmingham, Alabama. He served as a seminary professor for ten years and nine years with a mission agency. He is the author of numerous articles and books on missions including *Roland Allen: Pioneer of Spontaneous Expansion*, *Apostolic Church Planting*, *Discovering Church Planting*, *Strangers Next Door*, and *Pressure Points*. He is the co-author of *Developing a Strategy for Missions* and co-editor of *Missionary Methods: Research, Reflections, and Realities*. He blogs at jdpayne.org, hosts a podcast (Strike the Match), and may be found on Twitter @jd_payne.

**Steven Richard Rutt (PhD, University of Lancaster, UK)** is assistant professor of Biblical Studies at Arizona Christian University and adjunct professor of Intercultural Studies at Fuller Theological Seminary (Arizona). He is a priest in the Reformed Episcopal Church (Anglican Church of North America) and is a visiting professor of missiology at the Reformed Episcopal Seminary (Pennsylvania). He serves as president for Covenant Renewal Ministries, Inc. and represents this organization as a missionary teacher internationally. He is also the author of two volumes on Roland Allen's missiology (forthcoming with Lutterworth Press).

**Robert Schmidt (PhD, University of Washington)** taught at the Lutheran Seminary in Nigeria and later served as a campus pastor at Colorado State University and the University of Washington. He has taught theology and international relations at Concordia University in Portland and was named Dean of Theology in 1992. He directed a Lay Assistant Program providing word and sacrament ministries for churches without pastors in Alaska and the Pacific Northwest. He has also lectured on lay ministry in Germany, Japan, China, Kazakhstan, and India and continues to write on the subject.

# ACKNOWLEDGMENTS

One of the delights that come from being an author, or an editor in this case, is that every book has a unique origin. For me, the story behind this work is a fascinating tale.

Over the past several years, I have written and published extensively on the life and missiology of Roland Allen. In fact, he is one of a few individuals whom the Lord has used to influence my life and ministry. While in seminary, I encountered Hubert Allen's biography of his grandfather (the only book-length biography written to date), *Roland Allen: Pioneer, Priest, and Prophet*. This work was very helpful in understanding the man whose missiology had incredible influence on twentieth century and twenty-first century missionary practices.

As I write this section, Hubert's book rests on my desk, pages falling out from numerous readings and filled with small yellow and blue post-it notes displaying my note-taking skills. In an early reading of this book, I recall at least a couple of references to a set of unpublished Roland Allen papers housed at Oxford. One of these references was to a complete draft of a study titled *The Ministry of Expansion: The Priesthood of the Laity*. I recall thinking how great it would be to have a chance to read this work. However, while I did have a future plan to visit the UK, my travels would not take me near Oxford.

It was in 2010 that I started to consider a publication in honor of the one hundredth anniversary of the 1912 publication of *Missionary Methods: St. Paul's or Ours*. At this time, I seriously considered writing a biography on Roland Allen which would include travels to the UK and an opportunity to examine *The Ministry of Expansion*. However, the Lord did not allow for such plans to develop. Life and ministry commitments took priority over such research and writing endeavors. In 2012, I was blessed to publish *Roland Allen: Pioneer of Spontaneous Expansion*, addressing a great deal of his missiology and some of his biography, and also co-edit (with Craig Ott) *Missionary Methods: Research, Reflections, and Realities*, a publication in partnership with William Carey Library and the Evangelical Missiological Society to honor the centennial event.

My plans to work with *The Ministry of Expansion* faded until one summer. While at a Gulf of Mexico beach in Alabama, I received an email from a stranger with Hubert Allen copied in the correspondence. Hubert and I had communicated via email over the years, but I was not familiar with the sender: Chicagoan, John Mulholland.

In this email, John shared that he had been influenced by the work of Roland Allen and that he and Hubert were attempting to publish *The Ministry of Expansion*. But, unfortunately, the publishers they approached were not interested in this work. They asked if we could work together to get this document to the world.

Knowing that William Carey Library had an excellent reputation and an extensive history publishing mission books and resources, I approached them with the idea to produce an edited book comprised of a few chapters complimenting Roland Allen's manuscript, but a book in which Allen's work would be the heart of the project.

Their response was an enthusiastic "Yes!"

In light of this partnership and vision for this book, I begin offering thanks to the brothers and sisters of William Carey Library. It has been a great pleasure to work with Jeff Minard and his team. Melissa Hughes' skills for clarity and editorial work were amazing! Thank you for your Kingdom labors to bring to light this important manuscript in the history of missions.

My appreciation is also due to Robert Schmidt, Steven Rutt, and Robert Banks for their chapter contributions. These men are among the best Roland Allen scholars in the world. You will enjoy reading what they have written in this book. Steven was particularly helpful in providing wisdom and certain Allen documents not in my possession.

It is a pleasure and honor to serve as one of the pastors of The Church at Brook Hills in Birmingham, Alabama. Thank you for your willingness to follow the Word and take the gospel to the peoples of this world. Roland Allen's influence is upon much of our church planting efforts. And the reason for this is because Allen was a man of The Book. Rob Johnston is one church member deserving special appreciation. Rob spent several days with me slowly reading the two copies of Allen's manuscript and checking the electronic version for accuracy. He also helped me track down some needed library resources.

The staff at The Bodleian Library of the University of Oxford was especially helpful in providing me with copies of Allen's work. There are two in existence with some variations between them. Thank you, Lucy McCann, senior archivist, for your assistance.

Of course, much appreciation is due to Hubert Allen. He has done much to advance the church's understanding of Roland Allen's life and thought. Hubert's writings are balanced and do not read like hagiographies. He provided the two family photos used for this book. Until now, these have never been published. It has been a blessing learning from Hubert and working with him on this project.

I know to write "last but not least" and that I have "saved the best for last" is cliché. However, in this case, these are not trite expressions; they are significant truths. For a *major* part of the story behind this book involves the work of one man. In fact, there would be no story without him. So, a very special word of appreciation is due to John Mulholland, who works at the D'Angelo Law Library of the University of Chicago. John did yeoman's work by volunteering and carefully typing Allen's unpublished manuscript into an electronic document. In addition to this labor, he also checked Allen's citations and provided me with needed articles. The book you now have in your possession would not have been possible without John's vision, work, and desire for the world to have access to *The Ministry of Expansion*. Thank you, John!

# PART I
# BACKGROUND

# ROLAND ALLEN
Missiology and *The Ministry of Expansion*

J. D. Payne

I am frequently asked to give lectures on Roland Allen to seminary classes. Before I begin, I often ask the class if they have read any of Allen's writings. My general observations reveal that about 10 percent of a class will have read one of Allen's books, usually *Missionary Methods: St. Paul's or Ours?*. A second question, related to the first, is how many of the students have heard of Roland Allen before enrolling in the class. Usually, the only students who have heard of him are those who have read his writings.[1]

And, truth be told, I also was a seminary student when first exposed to Allen through *Missionary Methods: St. Paul's or Ours?*.

Irony is found in this scarcity of familiarity with Roland Allen. For Allen was one of the most influential individuals in missionary circles during the twentieth century. And his influence, at least among evangelicals, is even stronger in the twenty-first century and continues to grow. His writings shaped the thoughts and practices of individuals such as Lesslie Newbigin, Donald McGavran, and Ralph Winter. He is well respected among many leaders of mission agencies and networks. Allen's name is often referenced and revered in church planting conversations.

His influence has not been limited to missiologists. Many New Testament scholars reference him in their bibliographies as a result of his studies of the Apostle Paul. However, among those serving in pastoral and missionary roles, Allen remains largely unknown.

---

1. I have observed that there is even a lack of familiarity among young, evangelical Anglicans.

A few years ago, I wrote a blog post that included the following characteristics of the potential Roland Allen aficionado:
- you are interested in church planting movements
- you think about church multiplication
- you have strong convictions about the role of the Holy Spirit in missions
- you prefer contextualized church planting over paternalism
- you believe in raising up leaders from the harvest
- you believe that the New Testament has something to say regarding how we should be doing missionary work today

The point of this post was to help readers understand that while few of them had any knowledge about Allen, his influence had shaped their thoughts, lives, and ministries. Just as the sun provides a gravitational pull on the earth even when not seen during the night, Allen's influence is present and active even if they were not aware of him. From the grave, he speaks!

## MISSIOLOGY OF ROLAND ALLEN

While space will not permit a detailed explanation of Allen's missiological views, it is important the reader have some familiarity with his thinking about missions.[2] His thoughts were often consumed with what he described as the spontaneous expansion of the church—a potential reality he claimed missionaries feared. He wrote that it would be a "delight to think that a Christian travelling on his business, or fleeing from persecution, could preach Christ, and a church spring up as the results of his preaching."[3] Such a

---

2. For a detailed discussion of Allen's missiology, see my book *Roland Allen: Pioneer of Spontaneous Expansion* (n.p.: CreateSpace, 2012).

3. Roland Allen, *The Spontaneous Expansion of the Church and the Causes which Hinder It* (Grand Rapids, MI: William B. Eerdmans Publishing Company, 1962), 7.

modern-day, Antioch disciple making movement (Acts 11:19-21), uncontrolled by the church, was the "terror of missionaries."[4] While Allen was not opposed to order and heritage, he was quick to speak against the traditions, legalism, and control that interfered with disciple making, growth in Christ, leadership development, and church planting in the Majority World. Upon comparing the church's present-day missionary organizations and structures to those in the New Testament, he believed Western culture and tradition had trumped biblical necessities. And it was these contemporary developments that hindered the expansion of the church.

Disciple making that resulted in the birth of contextualized (*indigenous* was the common parlance in Allen's day) churches was a simple process that could lead to exponential church growth. He wrote:

> This then is what I mean by spontaneous expansion. I mean the expansion which follows the unexhorted and unorganized activity of individual members of the Church explaining to others the Gospel which they have found for themselves; I mean the expansion which follows the irresistible attraction of the Christian Church for men who see its ordered life, and are drawn to it by desire to discover the secret of a life which they instinctively desire to share; I mean also the expansion of the Church by the addition of new churches.[5]

Missionaries who brought a heavy amount of paternalism to the field, were missionaries who hindered such gospel advancement. Allen often wrote of Western missionaries who feared what

---

4. Roland Allen, "Spontaneous Expansion: The Terror of Missionaries." *World Dominion* 4 (1926): 218–24.

5. Ibid.

might happen if they were not governing and dictating all matters related to Majority World believers. He would argue against this fear and would call missionaries to orient their perspective to Christ and the power of his gospel. A missionary faith, not fear, was needed:

> We fear corruption and degeneration; when shall we cease to fear them? The roots of that fear are in us, and when shall we eradicate them, and how? There will always be cause for that fear, if we look at men. If we look at Christ then we may escape; but then why should we not escape now? He does not change. When we talk of a day when we shall be able to trust our converts in non-Christian lands, we are looking at them. So long as we look at them we shall be afraid.[6]

## THE WAY OF CHRIST

Though much of Allen's writings focused on the Apostle Paul, he understood that some members of the apostolic church had been discipled by Jesus and had been taught not to fear the possible outcome of their labors, but walk by faith. "He trained them in the work," Allen wrote, "not outside of it; in the world, not in a hothouse."[7]

And this training was to prepare them for his departure and the ongoing mission. The apostolic approach to disciple making and church multiplication originated with Jesus, not the Twelve or the Apostle Paul. According to Allen:

---

6. Roland Allen, "The Place of 'Faith' in Missionary Evangelism," *World Dominion* 8 (1930): 238.

7. Roland Allen, "New Testament Missionary Methods," *The Missionary Review of the World* 52 (1929): 21.

The Apostles followed Christ in this; they established a society, a spiritual society on earth. The establishment of this society is most clearly seen in the work and writing of the Apostle Paul. He recognized a Church; he established churches.[8]

This Christological (and thoroughly Trinitarian) understanding was also explained in his work *Pentecost and the World*. Reflecting on the Holy Spirit, he wrote:

> The same Holy Spirit which descended upon Christ was to descend upon them [apostles]. . . . Thus the work of the apostles with which this book is concerned is linked with the work of Jesus Christ as the carrying on of that which He began on earth under the impulse of the same Spirit through whom He acted and spoke.[9]

## PNEUMATOLOGY AND ECCLESIOLOGY

Understanding Allen's missiology requires grasping his thoughts regarding the Holy Spirit and the local church. John Branner was correct when he wrote that "the gift of the Holy Spirit to believers was something which was to govern Allen's entire concept of mission, particularly that of the indigenous church."[10] Charles Chaney suggested that Allen's understanding of the Spirit was

---

8. Ibid., 22.
9. Roland Allen, "*Pentecost and the World: the Revelation of the Holy Spirit in the 'Acts of the Apostles,'*" in *The Ministry of the Spirit: Selected Writings of Roland Allen*, American ed., edited by David M. Paton, (Grand Rapids, MI: William B. Eerdmans, 1962), 6.
10. John E. Branner, "Roland Allen: Pioneer in a Spirit-Centered Theology of Mission," *Missiology* 5 (1977): 181.

likely his "most important contribution to missiological theory and the most distinctive thrust of his thought."[11]

The Spirit was the one who led the church to do mission. He was the one who worked in the lives of new churches, sanctifying them as they awaited the return of the Lord. Missionaries were to teach these new believers how to rely on the Spirit. And missionaries had to manifest a faith in the power of the Spirit to protect, lead, and mature these churches.

Allen argued that the active role of the Spirit of mission was so strong that even if Jesus never gave the Great Commission, the church would still go into all the world and make disciples. "Had the Lord not given any such command," he noted, "had the Scriptures never contained such a form of words, or could Christians blot it out from their Bibles and from their memories, the obligation to preach the Gospel to all nations would not have been diminished by a single iota."[12] The spontaneous expansion of the church was dependent upon a Spirit-filled church. Such advancement was impossible without the active agency of the Spirit.

Allen's pneumatology and ecclesiology were woven together and unable to be separated. The Spirit was intimately connected to the church, and the church was dependent upon the Spirit for life, growth, and power. This relationship in Allen's missiology influenced his understanding of the indigenous nature of the church and the Eucharist.

Since churches came from people in a given context, those churches were to express themselves according to the cultures of those people. Churches in the West had developed structures, ministry styles, and organizations that missionaries often expected to be embraced by Majority World churches. However, Allen

---

11. Charles Chaney, "Roland Allen: The Basis of His Missionary Principles and His Influence Today," *Occasional Bulletin* 14, no. 5 (May 1963): 5.

12. Roland Allen, *Essential Missionary Principles* (New York, NY: Flemming H. Revell Company, 1913), 67.

had little patience for such expectations whenever Western cultural preferences trumped the application of biblical expectations to the mission field. These new churches were to be indigenous churches (i.e., contextualized) and did not need Western trappings. Whenever missionaries had expectations for churches to look like their Western counterparts, the spontaneous expansion would be hindered.

This complex ecclesiology was not helpful to Kingdom work. Though Allen was a high church Anglican, he recognized the biblical simplicity of the church:

> In the New Testament the idea of a Church is simple. It is an organized body of Christians in a place with its [leaders]. The Christians with their officers are the Church in the place, and they are addressed as such. This is simple and intelligible. That Church is the visible Body of Christ in the place, and it has all the rights and privileges and duties of the Body of Christ. Above it is the Universal Church, composed of all the Churches in the world, and of all the redeemed in heaven and on earth. The Apostolic idea of the Church is wonderfully intelligible to men everywhere.... The Apostolic system is so simple, that it can be apprehended by men in every stage of education, and civilization.[13]

This simplicity was often necessary for the church to come into existence in pioneer fields and multiply throughout people groups. An apostolic approach to the planting of churches required that new churches be indigenous and manifesting characteristics of

---

13. Roland Allen, "Devolution: The Question of the Hour," *World Dominion* 5 (1927): 283–84.

young congregations, rather than displaying characteristics of churches that were decades and even centuries old.

New churches were to come from the new believers, a practice Allen observed in the Scriptures:

> Now if we look at the work of St. Paul, I think it must be perfectly clear that the local Churches of his foundation were essentially what we call native Churches. The little groups of Christians that he established in towns like Lystra or Derbe, Thessalonica or Beroea, were wholly composed of permanent residents in the country. They managed their own internal affairs under the leadership of their own officers, they administered their own sacraments, they controlled their own finance, and they propagated themselves, establishing in neighbouring towns or villages Churches like themselves.[14]

Allen's convictions regarding their right to manage these internal affairs related to the administration of the Eucharist eventually resulted in his work *The Ministry of Expansion*. He believed "A body which cannot perform its own proper rites is not a Church."[15] But how was the native church to participate in the Eucharist if ordained clergy were not present?

---

14. Roland Allen, "The Essentials of an Indigenous Church," *World Dominion* 3 (1925): 111.

15. Roland Allen, "The Priesthood of the Church," *The Church Quarterly Review* 115 (1933): 237.

## ROLE OF THE MISSIONARY

There are at least four significant components to understanding Allen's missiology as related to missionaries. First, missionaries desiring the spontaneous expansion of the church were to follow an apostolic approach in their field labors. This meant that just as the Apostle Paul left new churches with the creed, sacraments, orders, and Scriptures, contemporary missionaries were to do likewise.[16] Allen understood that what he advocated was a radical idea. "Today," he wrote, "if a man ventures to suggest that there may be something in the methods by which St. Paul attained such wonderful results worthy of our careful attention, and perhaps of our imitation, he is in danger of being accused of revolutionary tendencies."[17]

The second important matter was that the missionary should give priority to evangelism. While many noble tasks could be pursued on the field, missionaries were not to give priority to social improvement or even be fixated on the number of converts. While Allen valued activities such as medical and educational missionary work, he argued that evangelistic missions met the "supreme need" in peoples' lives, asking "May I, then, take it as agreed that the evangelization is the supreme end of missions?"[18]

The third important function of missionaries, after disciples were made, was a practice he referred to as the ministration of the Spirit. This was so important that he described it as being the

---

16. Allen understood the creed to be a simple statement of faith that expressed the simple gospel and some fundamental truths Christians believed. Sacraments were the Eucharist and baptism. The Orders referred to church leadership.

17. Roland Allen, *Missionary Methods: St. Paul's or Ours?* (Grand Rapids, MI: William B. Eerdmans, 1962), 4.

18. Roland Allen, "The Relation between Medical, Educational, and Evangelistic Work in Foreign Missions," *Church Missionary Society* (March 1920), 58.

"goal" for missionaries and the "sole work of the missionary of the Gospel."[19] New churches needed to be dependent on the Spirit and not outsiders. Missionaries were to teach new believers how to follow the Spirit's leadership and be self-governing, self-propagating, and self-supporting. The local mission was not to devolve authority to the new churches over time. New churches could not carry out their ministries by proxy; they could not live the Christian life dependent upon the local mission. Rather, the churches had everything they needed to be the church from the moment of their births.

The way to follow an apostolic approach and avoid devolution after teaching about the Spirit was to set the churches free. He wrote:

> Just as we ourselves only manifest spirit in our activities where those activities are free and spontaneous, not forced or governed or controlled . . . so those to whom we minister the Spirit can only show forth His power in their own free spontaneous activity. Action done under compulsion or direction is not revelation of the Spirit. If we want to see what is the character of any living thing, we must see what it does in free conditions. To say that it is enough to see how it acts under ordered conditions is only to confuse our minds; because the manifestation of its character is made only so far as it is free under the ordered conditions. If

---

19. Roland Allen, *Mission Activities Considered in Relation to the Manifestation of the Spirit* (London: World Dominion Press, 1927), 30, 33. This booklet was later republished in Roland Allen, *The Ministry of the Spirit*, edited by David M. Paton (Grand Rapids, MI: William B. Eerdmans Publishing Company, 1960), 87–113. This statement that the ministration of the Spirit was the "sole work of the missionary," revealed Allen's integrated thinking. Unless the missionary gave priority to evangelism (i.e., "supreme end of missions"), the people, who would become disciples, would not be able to experience the ministration of the Spirit (i.e., missionary "goal").

then we want to see a manifestation of the Spirit in a form which can be understood, it must be in the unfettered activity of Christians under their own natural conditions.[20]

Finally, encompassing these three components to the role of the missionary was the notion of missionary faith. Missionaries had to have faith in the power of the Spirit and the Word of God to protect and build up the new churches. Allen wrote: "The fact is that our missionaries cannot, or will not, entrust the doctrine and the rites of the Christian faith to raw converts, in the simple faith that the Gospel can stand in its own strength. They act as if they thought that the religion which they preach could not stand in its own strength."[21] Anticipating his readers' thoughts of possible corruption that men and women might bring to the church, he noted that such thinking admits "that we do not believe that our Gospel is so powerful that it can of itself raise a fallen race."[22] Missionaries had to have this type of faith so they could retire from the ministry in this location and transition to another ministry context.

The spontaneous expansion of the church was a possibility when a Spirit-filled, indigenous church followed the commands of the Lord in her context while missionaries manifested missionary faith. Allen knew this idea was a simple concept in theory, but an extremely difficult reality to achieve due to Western church expectations. And it was church expectations related to ordination and the Eucharist that led Allen to write *The Ministry of Expansion: The Priesthood of the Laity*.

---

20. Ibid., 30–31.
21. Roland Allen, "The Place of 'Faith' in Missionary Evangelism," *World Dominion* 8 (1930): 237.
22. Ibid., 240.

## ALLEN AND *THE MINISTRY OF EXPANSION*

Colonialism was coming to an end during Allen's lifetime. Nevertheless, missionary activity still felt the strong grasp of paternalism. Having lived in China during the violent days of the Boxer Rebellion and through his global travels, Allen became troubled by missionary practices that were governed more by cultural expectations than biblical guidelines. He spent over half of his life calling the church back to the Bible.

His thoughts were not often well received. Like many thought leaders, he was ahead of his time. He spoke of matters that the church would eventually come to accept in the latter part of the twentieth century. It would not be an overstatement to note that Allen was a misunderstood prophet.

When his adolescent grandson approached him one day and inquired about reading his books, Allen responded, *"Oh, yes, you can read them by all means—but you won't understand them; I don't think anyone is going to understand them until I've been dead ten years."*[23] It was not a full decade following his death before people started taking his thoughts seriously, but it was close.

The reader who seeks to understand *The Ministry of Expansion: The Priesthood of the Laity* needs to understand Allen's background and life. There is no person on the planet more capable of sharing this biographical information than that grandson who was once encouraged to read Allen's writings. Hubert Allen's contribution to this book provides the reader with a glimpse into the world and life of the man behind *The Ministry of Expansion*.

Most readers expect a book to have some degree of relevance to life. We read to grow in knowledge and see things from a different perspective. Relevance is important. And it is this topic that Robert Schmidt addresses in his chapter. Schmidt assists

---

23. Hubert J. B. Allen, *Roland Allen: Pioneer, Priest, and Prophet* (Cincinnati, OH: Forward Movement Publications; Grand Rapids, MI: William B. Eerdmans, 1995), vii (emphasis in the original).

the reader in understanding the importance of *The Ministry of Expansion* to the twenty-first century church. He attempts to answer the question "Why publish such a book after all of these years?" Both readers from Anglican and non-Anglican traditions are challenged by this commentary. While Allen described the limitations of applying certain ecclesiological traditions of Christianized contexts to pioneer fields, many churches continue this unhealthy practice. Schmidt relates *The Ministry of Expansion* to four contemporary crises facing the church.

Allen was a prolific writer. Since he left us with numerous publications, the contemporary reader is able to trace the missiological developments in his works over the years. While his most popular and influential writings are *Missionary Methods: St. Paul's or Ours?* and *The Spontaneous Expansion of the Church*, both of these were published in 1912 and 1927, respectively. Allen's death was in June 1947. Therefore, his thoughts continued to evolve and develop during those twenty years.

The work you have in hand, *The Ministry of Expansion: The Priesthood of the Laity*, was likely written in the latter 1930s.[24] Several of Allen's published writings in the decade that preceded this manuscript addressed matters related to voluntary clergy and missionaries.[25] Though Allen was a high church Anglican,

---

24. Allen did not place a date on either of his two manuscripts. Hubert Allen shared that he thinks the book was written within a year or two of 1938. Email to editor, 13 May 2016.

25. His books included: *Voluntary Clergy* (London: S.P.C.K., 1923), *Voluntary Clergy Overseas: An Answer to the Fifth World Call* (Beaconsfield: privately printed, 1928), and *The Case for Voluntary Clergy* (London: Eyre and Spottiswoodie, 1940). Some of Allen's published articles from this period included: "Voluntary Service in the Mission Field," *World Dominion* 5 (1927): 135–43, "The Need for Non-Professional Missionaries," *World Dominion* 6 (1928): 195–201, "The Work of Non-Professional Missionaries," *World Dominion* 6 (1928): 298–304, "Voluntary Clergy and the Lambeth Conference," *The Church Overseas* (1931): 145–53, and "The Priesthood of the Church," *The Church Quarterly Review* 116 (1933): 234–44.

his writings were reflecting thoughts that dealt with important church and missionary activities in the Majority World where the Anglican Church did not have well-developed church structures and organizations. *The Ministry of Expansion* was no exception to this line of thought. For it is here that Allen makes the argument that the unordained should be permitted to officiate at the Communion table.

This thought was a radical idea. Only the individual who was able to complete the years of education and ordination requirements was eligible to administer the Lord's Supper. Allen, familiar with many Majority World contexts, recognized that if such tradition was followed, then it would be years (and in some locations, never) before certain churches would be able to participate in Communion with their own leadership.

As Steven Rutt addresses in his chapter, "Background and Overview of *The Ministry of Expansion*," Allen argued against the longstanding and well-respected teachings of two leading theologians: Robert Moberly and Charles Gore. Rutt's contribution to this book provides the reader with important historical context and summary of Allen's work. We are leaving the future researcher to determine whether or not Allen fairly explained and rebutted Moberly's and Gore's arguments. This book is not an attempt to critique Allen, but published to allow him to speak for himself.

*The Ministry of Expansion* was not the last of Allen's writings on this subject. In 1943, he wrote an untitled manuscript addressing the partaking of Communion within the home and with the head of the household overseeing this act. In this writing, he confessed that he and his wife had taken the bread and cup in this fashion. He also noted that he encouraged others to do so as well. David M. Paton later published this writing and provided a title: *The Family Rite*. This was published in his edited book *Reform of the Ministry: A Study in the Work of Roland Allen*. Several years later, Paton and Charles H. Long co-edited *The Compulsion of the Spirit: A Roland Allen Reader*. In this book, they published *The*

*Family Rite*, with a significantly reduced length from the original Allen document.[26]

The reader is encouraged to read *The Family Rite* to understand the development of Allen's thought that followed his writing of *The Ministry of Expansion*. At the time of this book's publication, *Reform of the Ministry* is still in print with Lutterworth Press.

However, before obtaining *The Family Rite*, one should read Robert Banks' postscript in this book. Banks' contribution serves as a valuable linchpin connecting Allen's thoughts in *The Ministry of Expansion* to those in *The Family Rite*. His work provides a helpful introduction to the 1943 Allen writing.

---

26. David M. Paton, ed., *Reform of the Ministry: A Study in the Work of Roland Allen* (London: Lutterworth Press, 1968) and David Paton and Charles H. Long, eds., *The Compulsion of the Spirit: A Roland Allen Reader* (Grand Rapids, MI: William B. Eerdmans Publishing Company; Cincinnati, OH: Forward Movement Publications, 1983).

# ROLAND ALLEN
## A Biographical Note

Hubert Allen

Fundamental to Roland Allen's ideas was one paramount concept, identified by Harry Boer as "the high and lofty significance which Allen ascribed to the Holy Spirit."[1] This concept led him to many conclusions.

His daughter once remarked of his career that "There are three themes in the life of Roland Allen which overlap like the tunes in a fugue."[2] First, he challenged contemporary methods in the mission field. Next he took issue with the Church of England's acquiescence to secular law. Finally he came to consider seriously destructive a belief which has long been fundamental for sacramental churches (e.g., Roman Catholics, Eastern Orthodox, Anglicans, and Lutherans): their interpretation of the doctrine of "Apostolic Succession."

It was this third theme that preoccupied my grandfather during the last three decades of his life, and it is this with which *The Ministry of Expansion* is concerned. In this chapter, I shall attempt to dwell only on those incidents and encounters which bear directly on this theme. For a fuller account of Roland's life I must refer readers to my book, *Roland Allen: Pioneer, Priest, and Prophet*.[3]

---

1. Harry R. Boer, "Roland Allen, the Holy Spirit and Missions," *World Dominion* 33, no. 5 (September–October 1955): 299.
2. Priscilla M. Allen, "Roland Allen—A Prophet for this Age," *The Living Church* 192, no. 16 (April 20, 1986): 11.
3. Hubert J. B. Allen, *Roland Allen: Pioneer, Priest, and Prophet* (Grand Rapids, MI: William B. Eerdmans; Cincinnati, OH: Forward Movement Publications, 1995).

Roland was born on 29 December 1868 in Derbyshire, England where his father was the ordained headmaster of St. Clement's School in Radbourne. But before his fifth birthday, his father—still not forty years old—died in British Honduras, probably of yellow fever. His mother, Priscilla, was very much the most significant influence on Roland throughout his childhood. She was one of the many daughters of the Reverend Joseph Henry Malpas, for more than fifty years the Vicar of Awre in Gloucestershire.

Although left with very little money, Priscilla successfully raised six of her seven children to adulthood with no more than the help of a devoted young nurse/housemaid from Somerset. Priscilla was a very devout and prayerful evangelical Anglican. In later life, Roland seemed to have been thinking of his mother when he remarked that he considered "profoundly true" the concept of "experimental religion"—that is to say "religion based upon a personal experience . . . of the reality of such great doctrines . . . as the indwelling of the Holy Ghost."[4]

The four Allen boys all succeeded in earning scholarships to schools in Bath and Bristol, and then to university. In 1887, although diagnosed with a weak heart, Roland entered Oxford's St John's College to read Classical "Mods," with History finals.[5] He won the Lothian Prize for a study of Pope Silvester II, and graduated with second class honors in 1890.

Although not studying theology for his degree, Roland was a founding member and the first honorary secretary of the Origen Society, an undergraduate group dedicated to examining theological ideas. He was moreover profoundly influenced by some of

---

4. Roland Allen, *Educational Principles and Missionary Methods* (London: Robert Scott, 1919), 103.

5. "Honour Moderations" was the term given to Part 1 of Oxford's Master's degree course (Greek and Latin philosophy), leading to Part 2, "Greats," in Classics and Philosophy, but could be other subjects. For Allen, Part 2 was historical studies.

the Anglo-Catholic scholars in Pusey House, just across the street from St John's. So when, like his elder brothers, he decided to study for Holy Orders in the Church of England, it was these influences, rather than his mother's "low church" persuasion, that led him to enter the High Anglican clergy training school in Leeds.

Roland's ambition since childhood had been to enter the overseas mission field. After serving his curacy, he managed in 1893 to persuade the Church of England's Mission to North China to recruit him, notwithstanding his heart condition. He arrived in Peking (Beijing) early in 1895, with the tasks both of acting as chaplain for the British Legation (as the UK embassy was termed) and—since he very quickly learned Mandarin (becoming "a 3,000-character man")—opening a clergy school for indigenous Chinese catechists at the Anglican mission in the southwest quarter of the Tartar city.

His experiences following this time, including exciting activities during the siege of the Legations during the Boxer Uprising of 1900, have little bearing on this present study, apart from the fact that "During those five years I became more and more uneasy in my mind."[6] What made him so uneasy was a growing conviction that, although foreigners could be very helpful to the Chinese in providing skills, they were *not* well fitted to be evangelists. Moreover, it was believed by the vast majority of Chinese that "all foreigners were Christians, and all Christians were to be judged by the actions of those whom they happened to meet"[7]— whether businessmen, merchants, engineers, diplomats or anyone

---

6. Roland Allen's address to the Swanwick conference of the Church Missionary Society, printed in *Church Missionary Review* (June 1927), n.p.

7. See Roland Allen, "Of Some of the Causes which Led to the Siege of the Foreign Legations at Peking," *Cornhill Magazine* 491 (November 1900); "Of Some of the Causes which Led to the Preservation of the Foreign Legations in Peking," *Cornhill Magazine* 492 (December 1900); and "Of Some of the Conclusions which May be Drawn from the Siege of the Foreign Legations in Peking," *Cornhill Magazine* 494 (February 1901).

else, and "an idea took root and quickly spread that to become a Christian involved submission to foreign domination."[8]

These thoughts evidently impressed his bishop (Charles Perry Scott). So, when Roland returned to China in late 1902 (after an extended furlough, during which he married Beatrice Tarleton, an admiral's daughter who had been working in London for several years for the Peking Medical Mission), Bishop Scott posted him some fifty miles south of the capital to the mission station of Yung-Ch'ing, and immediately, with Scott's approval, he began to experiment with some of his radical ideas, on the lines he was to set out nearly ten years later in the epilogue of his first controversial book—*Missionary Methods: St Paul's or Ours?*.

Roland was able to report that "The Bishop is heartily in sympathy with me"; but sadly (as it seemed to everyone), after a few months his health again deteriorated seriously, and the doctors ordered him to go home to England, with his wife and three-month-old daughter.[9] In fact, half a century later his influence in China proved by no means to have ceased: "As the Anglican and Protestant Chinese Christians made their accommodations . . . developing the Three-Self Movement as the principal vehicle of the Churches' existence and survival," Roland was "the one non-Chinese thinker whose theological understanding of Three-Self" they referred to "again and again."[10]

Back in England, Roland recovered quite quickly, but he was forbidden to return to China, so the next theme in the "fugue" began with his appointment as vicar to Chalfont St Peter, midway between Oxford and London, and in those days still a

---

8. Lamin Sanneh, *Disciples of All Nations: Pillars of World Christianity* (Oxford: Oxford University Press, 2007), 224.

9. Roland Allen, title unknown, *The Land of Sinim* 11, no. 4 (October 1903): 18.

10. Daniel O'Connor, ed., *Three Centuries of Mission: The United Society for the Propagation of the Gospel 1701–2000* (London: Bloomsbury Academic, 2000), 134.

predominantly rural parish. He greatly enjoyed the work of a busy country parson, and this was the happiest period of Beatrice's life. Their son—my father—was born there in November 1904.

But once again Roland soon began to feel uneasy. The Church of England was the lawfully "established" church of the nation, and in consequence every person in the land had the legal right to be baptized, married, and buried in accordance with full Christian rites—even persons who "habitually neglect their religious duties, or openly deny the truth of the Creeds, or by the immorality of their lives openly defy the laws of God."[11] For Roland, for whom the Christian sacraments were sacred and supreme, this was intolerable, demanding "the acquiescence of a priest in a practice which he cannot justify." Although puzzled that "a great many good and thoughtful men . . . perform these offices without reproach," he felt very strongly that "law cannot justify impiety, and it is impiety to take God's Holy Name in vain." He resigned during Christmastide in 1907. Although emphasizing that, far from forsaking the church, he was "protesting against a misuse of her rites; to her principles I am profoundly attached." The final theme in his "fugue," began with the farewell speech to his parishioners. Roland noted that "the Church would go forward more and more . . . as they realized more and more that the work of the Church was not the work of the individual priest, but it was the church of the laity, and not merely the church of the clergy."[12]

---

11. Unless otherwise noted, all quotations in this paragraph are from Roland's "Letter to the Parishioners of Chalfont St. Peter," 25 November, 1907 and reprinted in Allen, *Roland Allen: Pioneer, Priest, and Prophet*, appendix 2 and in David M. Paton, ed., *The Ministry of the Spirit: Selected Writings of Roland Allen* (Grand Rapids, MI: William B. Eerdmans, 1960), 191–97.

12. Roland Allen, *Foundation Principles of Foreign Missions* (Suffolk: Richard Clay and Sons, 1910). The only surviving copy of this privately printed book I know of was evidently annotated by Roland and much more by his wife, Beatrice. I assume Roland decided not to proceed with publication, but to go on to write the much more elaborate *Missionary Methods* of 1912.

Roland seemed to have realized much earlier than most people that the Church of England's parochial system, depending on at least one resident priest in every parish, would soon start to disintegrate for many reasons: partly because the drift to the cities was leading to more urban churches, all of which needed staff, at a time when fewer and fewer men were being attracted to the ministry, and partly because the church was ceasing to be the focal point of every community. Occasional visits by callow young men, fresh from clergy training colleges, with time to do little more than conduct one or two services, was very far from being an adequate substitute for mature resident incumbents, with time to get to know each and every family, and to appreciate and often to help them with their problems. In the absence of a permanent vicar or rector, villagers were obliged instead to turn more and more for help and advice to other worthies, such as the postmistress or the landlord of the local hostelry.

After his resignation (which meant he could no longer obtain any regular work as an incumbent Anglican priest), the family relied for several years on Beatrice's meagre inherited wealth, supplemented by Roland occasionally acting to relieve sick clergy, or doing deputation work for overseas missions. But he spent this period in much study—reading and reflecting particularly on the New Testament and the works of Adolf von Harnack and of W. M. Ramsay (a professor in Oxford's Exeter College, where Roland's brother Willoughby was Chaplain).

The first fruit of these studies was a booklet printed in 1910, but never published. In this work, Roland declared his dedication to "the high and lofty significance of the Holy Spirit." This conviction was noted with statements such as "we are missionaries

---

This extant copy was presumably kept by my grandmother, when most of Roland's own papers were handed over to the Survey Application Trust, and thence, via the United Society for the Propagation of the Gospel, to the Bodleian Library at Oxford.

of the Gospel, not of the law; we administer the Spirit, not the letter."[13]

Toward the end of 1910, he and Beatrice contrived to widen his experience of overseas missions by a visit to India, where he was invited to preach in several major cities, and—more significantly—he became acquainted with both Bishop Henry Whitehead of Madras and the future Bishop of Dornakal, V. S. Azariah. These two men respectively would later write laudatory forewords for Roland's two most successful publications: *Missionary Methods: St. Paul's or Ours?* and *The Spontaneous Expansion of the Church*.[14]

*Missionary Methods*, published in 1912, caused a considerable stir in church circles. However, Roland was disappointed and frustrated that, even though several people he admired acknowledged the force of his arguments, they remained impervious to the need for change. The book deeply impressed Sidney James Wells Clark, a wealthy clothing manufacturer, who had been horrified during business voyages to the Far East to observe the wastefulness and inefficiency of overseas missions. However, Clark was ill-educated and failed to impress any of the missionary societies. So, early in 1914, he sought Roland and began discussions with him of how they could partner together for global missions.

The two of them were side-tracked by World War I. Clark worked with refugees in Belgium and undertook sundry "disagreeable" voluntary jobs in London. Roland was invalided out of the Royal Navy (after swimming ashore in October 1914 from the wrecked hospital ship on which he had been serving as Chaplain) and spent most of the rest of the war teaching classics at a school in Worcester. However, as early as 1917, the two men reunited and

---

13. Ibid., 63.
14. Roland Allen, *Missionary Methods: St Paul's or Ours? A Study of the Church in the Four Provinces* (London: Robert Scott, 1912) and *The Spontaneous Expansion of the Church: And the Causes which Hinder It* (London: World Dominion Press, 1927). Roland's children irreverently nicknamed these two works, "Mish-Meth" and "Sponx," respectively.

were joined by Dr. Thomas Cochrane, freshly retired from work with the Peking Union Medical College. The three men quickly established the "World Dominion Movement," dedicated to:
1. the Lord Jesus Christ and the centrality of His cross;
2. the Bible as the final authority on faith and practice;
3. the Lord's command to worldwide witness.[15]

During the following twelve years—in the Movement's revised form as the Survey Application Trust, together with its World Dominion Press—the Trust published a quarterly journal, as well as books, surveys, and numerous pamphlets, which together provided outlets through which Roland could freely voice his own ideas and comment on relevant contemporary events and publications. Moreover, Clark provided Roland with a house[16] and a small annual salary, so he could devote his undivided attention to research and to the propagation of his ideas.

Nevertheless, in spite of their shared "deep concern for the place and pre-eminence of the Holy Spirit," friction emerged between the three men.[17] Roland took no interest in the systematic surveys of worldwide missionary activities, which were the primary interest and concern of both Clark and Cochrane. Although bored by his colleagues' surveys, Roland had no scruples with using the Trust's funds for extensive travel.

A journey of several months in 1924 to study the shortcomings of the Archbishops' Western Canada Fund brought home to

---

15. The World Dominion Movement was a term used to cover all of the activities of the Survey Application Trust—a ministry to conduct missionary research across the world—and its publishing arm, World Dominion Press. See Kenneth Grubb, "The Story of the Survey Application Trust," in David M. Paton, ed., *Reform of the Ministry: A Study in the World of Roland Allen* (London: Lutterworth Press, 1968), 69.

16. The house was called "Amenbury" and located in Beaconsfield, a town west of London.

17. Alexander McLeish, "Biographical Memoir," in David M. Paton, ed., *The Ministry of the Spirit: Selected Writings of Roland Allen* (Grand Rapids, MI: William B. Eerdmans Publishing Company, 1960), xii.

him the plight of many devout Christians, who were isolated by distance from any church or priest, so that months or even years could pass by without their having any access to the church's Sacraments. This phenomenon was to preoccupy Roland for the rest of his life, especially because he also observed it frequently when he went on additional travels for the Trust to Northern Rhodesia, South Africa, and India. He even encountered it during his retirement in East Africa.

As nonconformists, neither the Congregationalist Clark nor the Methodist Cochrane shared Roland's high church concern for the sacraments and for the Church of England's faltering stipendiary system. In consequence, when he first began to concentrate on addressing these themes in a small book entitled *Voluntary Clergy Overseas*, Cochrane withdrew consent for its publication through the Trust even though the World Dominion Press printed the book. Roland was then obliged to publish the printed copies privately. Thus when he developed his arguments in a substantial book—*The Case for Voluntary Clergy*—he had to turn to a completely different publisher.[18]

What had dawned on Roland was the conviction that the New Testament requires two very different forms of Christian leadership. On the one hand, there was a need for evangelists and preachers to spread the Word. In order to guard against error, these people needed to be thoroughly instructed in the faith either by persons trained by the apostles, or subsequently by persons trained by them and their direct successors (e.g., as Paul taught Timothy and Titus). But alongside these learned evangelists there was a need in every locality for competent persons to provide the sacraments, which Jesus commanded all his followers to observe. Such people needed to be elders, respected by the whole community. They did not need detailed understanding of abstruse theological doctrines, but rather were required by Paul

---

18. Roland published with Eyre and Spottiswoode of London in 1930.

simply to have the qualities set out in his letters to Timothy and Titus.[19] Once Paul was satisfied that such people had been identified in a locality, he was content to leave the local church in their hands—although sometimes returning to visit or sending them an admonitory letter when they seemed to be going astray.

Roland believed the church had mistakenly, during the many centuries when few but the clergy were literate, fused together these two very different roles, so that presiding at the Eucharist had become unnecessarily restricted to persons who had undergone extensive theological training. Although appropriate and necessary for those charged with preaching and evangelism, such thorough academic training was quite unnecessary for respected elders leading worship in local churches. In a similar vein, Roland cited approvingly Father Herbert Kelly's ridicule of "the familiar absurdity of the lay reader . . . that the man who may not celebrate, because he is too uneducated and has not passed examinations, is allowed to preach and minister to souls!"[20]

Roland did not question the church's continuing need for professional clergy—persons who could, in addition to full-time priestly duties in more populous parishes, follow Paul in providing pastoral oversight for the less trained local lay ministers. They would provide the essential leadership roles, such as bishops and other officers. Roland was dwelling on the plight of persons living in remote regions, where they were unlikely to see an ordained priest for months or years—if ever. In such circumstances, the church should follow Paul's example by ordaining laymen (i.e., respected elders) without requiring them to undergo the lengthy theological training rightly required of preachers and evangelists.[21]

---

19. See 1 Timothy 3:1–7 and Titus 1:6–9.

20. Roland Allen citing *The East & the West*, (April 1916), 435, in his book *The Spontaneous Expansion of the Church, and the Causes which Hinder It* (London: World Dominion Press, 1927), 175.

21. Roland's arguments have a much wider significance, because if this policy were accepted in principle, it could clearly lead to solving the Church

By the early 1930s, Roland's son and daughter-in-law were teaching in East Africa, where his daughter also found work as a librarian. He and Beatrice immigrated to Nairobi, Kenya, where they settled down for the rest of his life. He continued to pursue his case for lay voluntary clergy, but the local Anglican bishops had no patience with his arguments—although they made use of him from time to time as locum for clergy who were sick or absent on furlough. He was also often asked to preside at friends' weddings or baptisms.

Roland soon found other interests—notably, learning Swahili and translating several epic poems from classical Swahili verse (a subject in which his son had become a noted authority) into English. He kept up a voluminous newspaper correspondence. During World War II, he worked to help Germans and Italians who had been interned. He died in June 1947 and is buried in Nairobi's City Park.[22] But from beyond that grave his message remains the same: *Forget the distortions of two millennia, and go back to our Christian Book of Instructions.*

---

of England's parochial problems: for even in the smallest and most remote parishes there should almost always be found at least one respected and devout lay pillar of the community, who could be instructed simply in the consecration and administration of the sacraments. Moreover, like Luke and Paul, Roland lived an era of male dominance. But, like them, he greatly admired the insight and integrity of many women—whether housewives in Macedonia, wives of tea-planters in Assam, or Swahili poets in East Africa. I am confident that he would have rejoiced to see women as bishops and among the ordained pillars of the community.

22. Beatrice survived him by twelve years and is buried in Kampala, where both of their children were by that time working at the University of East Africa at Makerere.

# THE MINISTRY OF EXPANSION AND CONTEMPORARY CRISES
Robert Schmidt

Why publish a book written by a missiologist who has been dead for over fifty years? Why? Because the crisis continues. There are simply too few ordained ministers for too many parishes and small groups of Christians seeking to worship their Lord. As a young missionary to Nigeria in the 1960s, I was assigned ten churches in addition to teaching at a seminary. Most of the missionaries served thirty churches, and one was responsible for sixty. A quick survey at that time showed that throughout the world there was one ordained pastor for every fourteen congregations.

## NOT ENOUGH PASTORS

With the education and placement of national pastors in Africa and Asia, many more congregations are being served with seminary graduates. However, in countries like Nigeria and Ethiopia, there is still only one ordained clergyman for every three or four parishes and even less in rural areas.[1] With the rapid expansion of the faith in China to an estimated 67 million Christians in China,[2] there are many Christian communities, especially in the numerous house churches, without a seminary-trained pastor. In India,

---

1. "The Lutheran Church of Nigeria," http://www.lcms.org/page.aspx?pid=1335 (accessed 10 April, 2015). Mekane Yesus, Ethiopia, http://en.wikipedia.org/wiki/Ethiopian_Evangelical_Church_Mekane_Yesus (accessed 10 April 2015).

2. "Global Christianity," Pew Research Center, http://www.pewforum.org/interactives/global-christianity/#/China,ALL (accessed 10, April 2015).

there are a growing number of non-baptized believers in Christ or Christ Bhaktas who are not members of organized congregations but worship in their homes or other smaller gatherings.[3] With the growing shortage of Roman Catholic priests in the West, there are probably even more Christian groups without the regular services of an ordained pastor.

In the unrecognized Christian communities in China and India, there often is no celebration of the Eucharist, or if so, it would hardly be accepted by more traditional Christian churches. Even when a seminary-trained pastor is available and serves a number of congregations, the entire nature of the ministry is changed. It is difficult to develop a strong pastoral relationship with most of the people; there is little time for teaching and instruction. Because the ordained minister is the only one permitted to perform sacramental functions, it means that the chief task of the ordained minister is to baptize and celebrate the Lord's Supper. The seminary education preparing the minister to preach and teach is relegated to the background, while saying the simple words during baptism and the Lord's Supper become all-important. Sitting in front of the young missionary, who may have had to memorize the words of institution in a foreign language, are often esteemed elders who previously conducted elaborate four-day rituals for the village. Yet, the young clergyman has the authority to celebrate the Sacrament and they do not. When the ordained minister is not around, there simply is no sacramental worship and in some cases that absence goes on for months and even years.

Roland Allen addressed this crisis in his own time with numerous books and articles. Several of his most famous works were *Missionary Methods: St. Paul's or Ours*[4] and *The Spontaneous*

---

3. Herbert Hoefer has compiled significant statistics in his book, *Churchless Christianity* (Pasadena: William Carey Library, 2001).

4. Roland Allen, *Missionary Methods: St. Paul's or Ours* (London: World Dominion Press, 1912).

*Expansion of the Church and the Causes which Hinder it.*[5] In his writings he argued that church authorities should recognize and enable local elders of congregations to conduct a full ministry of Word and Sacrament. Largely because of his writings, there have been moves in many denominations and across the world to bless the ministry of the laity and authorize lay people to baptize and preside at the Eucharist.

Such moves, however, continue to meet strong objections. One recently publicized controversy took place in the Anglican Province of New South Wales in Australia. While the synod called for the lay presidency at the Eucharist to be permitted when no priest was available, it met with strong objections from the Archbishop of Canterbury and others in Australia.[6] In a book on the subject, Nicolas Taylor, quoting Bishop Robert Moberly, continues to oppose the practice of a lay celebration of the Eucharist.[7] Allen was well acquainted with these objections and set out to write a book dealing with them. This is how the heretofore unpublished, *The Ministry of Expansion: The Priesthood of the Laity* came to be written. Now, as the positions of Charles Gore and Moberly are again cited to prohibit the lay presidency at the Eucharist, Allen's voice in this small volume almost comes as a voice from the dead to argue for it.

Roland Allen came out of the "high church" tradition of the Anglican Communion with its great respect for the office of the ministry. As a student he had been inspired by his mentor, Charles Gore, the then Principal of Pusey House, later to become the Bishop of Oxford. In 1919 Allen asked Bishop Gore to write the introduction to Allen's book, *Educational Principles*

---

5. Roland Allen, *The Spontaneous Expansion of the Church and the Causes which Hinder It* (Grand Rapids, MI: William B. Eerdmans, 1927).

6. John Davis, http://web.stpeters.org.au/presidency/laypresupdate.shtml (accessed 10 April, 2015).

7. Nicolas Taylor, *Lay Presidency at the Eucharist: An Anglican Approach* (London: Mowbray, 2009), 123.

*and Missionary Methods.*[8] Although Gore penned the Introduction, it was already clear that there were some tensions between his perspective, formed in the settled, organized church, and the insights of the missionary who had been forced to see things differently. Possibly referring to the position advocated by Allen, Gore wondered about the modern lack of the "dogmatic" element in education.

In *The Ministry of Expansion: The Priesthood of the Laity* the stress between Allen's position and the arguments of Gore and Moberly are brought to the breaking point. Yet Allen is careful not to make a radical split with the entire tradition with which he had been raised. In each chapter Allen is careful not to deny the basic points made by Gore and Moberly. Rather, he argues time and again, those arguments are not applicable in a situation without ordained clergy.

Partly inspired by the insights of Allen and by the sheer magnitude of ministering to isolated groups in Alaska, a group of Lutheran congregations in Alaska in the 1990s began training lay people to lead worship, baptize, and preside at Communion services. At the same time some former missionaries sought to legitimize that practice through a resolution to their district, creating a lay ministry program. When it was clearly seen by the district that in Alaska it was a choice between lay ministry and no ministry at all, the lay program received the blessing of the district.[9] In a bittersweet moment several years later I witnessed a young Anglican priest handing over a Native American parish in Alaska to the care of a Lutheran lay minister. Since there were no ordained clergy available and none would be available in the future, it was all he could do.

---

8. Charles Gore, "Introduction" in Roland Allen, *Educational Principles and Missionary Methods* (London: Robert Scott, 1919).

9. Hans Spalteholz, Matthew L. Becker, and Dwaine Charles Brandt, eds., *God Opens Doors: Centennial Celebration of the Northwest District of the Lutheran Church-Missouri Synod* (Portland: Northwest District, 2000), 73, 257.

As much as Allen carefully wished to build his case for lay people to preside at the Eucharist where no priest is available, his opponents then and now know that if the lay presidency is permitted where no priests are available, what is to prevent a lay presidency at the Eucharist even when ordained clergy are available? And, if that is permitted, will it not call into question the whole identity, prerogatives, and even financial support of the clergy also in the organized church?

This has become still more of an issue in the years since *The Ministry of Expansion* was written. At the time when Allen wrote, there were huge areas of Africa, Asia, North America, and Australia where there were no ordained clergy. Despite the continuing lack of clergy in places like Alaska, opponents might argue that there are fewer of those geographical areas now than there were at his time of writing. Since then, however, a number of other crises have challenged the traditional views of church and ministry.

## THE CULTURAL CRISIS

Christian leaders who have had the greatest appreciation of Roland Allen have been those ministering to people of widely different cultures. In Tanzania, the Roman Catholic priest, Vincent Donovan, inspired by Allen, helped the Masai people come to their own understanding of baptism and the Eucharist. Donovan was impressed by the communal orientation of the Masai. In that context what would the ministry of Word and Sacrament look like? He asks:

> They must be able to preach in their services and liturgies. They must be able securely to deepen the understanding of the church—didache. They must be able to bring down blessing on their human lives, making sacred the symbols and signs by which they live. They must be able to effect conversion and partake of and dispense

forgiveness of sin. They must be able to break bread together to build up the body of Christ.[10]

For Donovan, candidates for the priesthood were together an illiterate elder, a younger elder who could read and write, a woman gifted in singing and explaining the message to non-Christians, one who was a good preacher and another a good pray-er. In that context together they would constitute the ministry, the priesthood of the church.[11]

In Columbia, Bruce Olson named "Bruchko" by the Moltilone people, worked five years seeking to understand their language and culture. Only in the midst of a crisis, when they were looking for a god they had lost, was he able to share the good news of Christ who had found them. Once that opening had been made he was able to share with them many other aspects of the faith. This was a process that had taken years. Yet, in only a short time the Moltilone people were able to communicate the faith to many of the tribes that surrounded them, some with whom they had previously been at war.[12] Allen's argument that the natural leaders of a people can many times better communicate the gospel than can a seminary-educated foreigner was well demonstrated.[13]

In India, Swami Dayanand Bharati, a serious student of Roland Allen, is notable among a growing number of Christ Bhaktas, previously called non-baptized believers in Christ. Historically, most Indians who became Christians and joined the missionary churches were Dalits or Harijans who were outcastes within Indian society. Many of those of the upper castes have been reluctant to give up their Hindu culture, and given the social

---

10. Vincent Donovan, *Christianity Rediscovered* (New York: Orbis Books, 1978), 116.
11. Ibid., 114.
12. Bruce Olson, *Bruchko* (Lake Mary, FL: Charisma House, 1973), 120–141.
13. *Missionary Methods*, 165.

compositions of these Christian congregations, they would not join them.[14] However, many have come to faith in Jesus through their experiences in visions, healings, and answers to prayers that have prompted them to accept Jesus as their personal Lord.

As a Christ Bhakta, Bharati wishes to have the Christian faith developed in an Indian framework. He writes:

> God used both the Jewish culture and religious system to reveal his truth to humanity. And his apostles used the Greek philosophy and terms to convey the same message to the Gentiles. Now to present the same truth to Indians, we should use the Indian framework.[15]

Furthermore, Bharati suggests that organized religion will never appeal to an average Hindu. Like Allen, he says that we must follow the pattern of spontaneity seen in the early church. Since all gathering requires some kind of coordination, the appointing of elders and deacons in the New Testament is understandable, and he believes the equivalent leadership roles will develop in the Hindu context.[16] For Christ Bhaktas, baptism is a family rite Bharati calls *diksha*.[17] For Holy Communion, the Christ Bhaktas celebrate their own *prasad* an Indian word that means grace.[18] Done in the home or a small gathering, leadership in this celebration naturally arises from the group.[19]

---

14. Herbert Hoefer, "Forward" in Dayanand Bharati, *Living Water and Indian Bowl: An Analysis of Christian Failings in Communicating Christ to Hindus, with Suggestions Toward Improvements* (Pasadena: William Carey Library, 2004), i-vii.

15. Bharati, *Living Water in Indian Bowl*, 29.

16. Ibid., 41–42.

17. Ibid., 90.

18. Ibid., 88.

19. Ibid., 51.

Meeting the cultural crisis with Allen's *The Ministry of Expansion* is not only true of overseas venues; it is also true for the United States. A ministry to African immigrants in the United States within one denomination revealed that only eight ordained pastors were serving ninety-two different congregations. In my own experience working with an Oromo (from central and southern Ethiopia) congregation in the Pacific Northwest, the church is thriving with five lay leaders who take turns preaching and leading in worship. Services are in the Oromo language; Oromo choirs introduce new music for Sunday morning services. Were the congregation to have waited for an ordained Oromo-speaking pastor, they may never have begun, nor would they have grown as fast numerically or spiritually.

## THE FINANCIAL CRISIS

A second crisis challenging the traditional conception of the church and ministry is financial. Many small congregations simply cannot afford a paid ordained pastor. It is reported that since 1969, 1,500 church buildings in England have closed after centuries of use.[20] *The Wall Street Journal* reports:

> The Church of England closes about 20 churches a year. Roughly 200 Danish churches have been deemed nonviable or underused. The Roman Catholic Church in Germany has shut about 515 churches in the past decade.[21]

---

20. Ken Ham and Brit Beemer, *Already Gone: Why Your Kids Will Quit Church and What You Can Do to Stop It* (Green Forest AR: Master Books, 2009), 10.

21. Naftali Bendavid, "Europe's Empty Churches Go on Sale," *The Wall Street Journal*, 2 January, 2015. https://www.wsj.com/articles/europes-empty-churches-go-on-sale-1420245359

In the United States, the crisis is also critical. Rural churches that cannot obtain the services of a retired pastor or share a pastor with several other parishes will have to close. Even those congregations that do obtain the services of a seminary graduate know that the young cleric will leave for greener pastures after a year or two. In urban areas, the situation is not much better. In many urban congregations the membership has eroded with flight to the suburbs and the aging of its most committed members. Now a small group meets in a cavernous sanctuary seeking to reach out to their community while supporting a pastor and keeping the building in repair. However, in both rural and urban areas, outreach and social concern for their communities are sapped by the financial burden in supporting an ordained pastor. Almost unnoticed is the fact that most denominations are having a difficult time in financing new missions and carrying out specialized ministries at universities, in institutional ministries, and in inner cities.

Closely connected with the financial crisis of keeping churches open is the concomitant problem of having enough pastors to serve the parishes that remain. Several years ago while I was in Baden-Württemberg in Germany, the notice came that the government there could no longer afford to support the number of theological students about to graduate. This would mean that many smaller parishes would no longer be served by their own pastor, and pastors in larger parishes would have to work alone in blessing marriages, performing confirmations, and burying people.

In England, the Anglican Church is facing a growing shortage of priests. The number of full-time clergy is predicted to fall to just seven thousand in ten years' time. The total number of clergy is declining by an average of about one hundred a year. In some parts of the nation clergy could find themselves overseeing clusters of twenty or more parishes with the help of laity.[22]

---

22. Jonathan Petre, "Church to Tackle Shortage of Vicars," *The Telegraph*, 6 August, 2007. http://www.telegraph.co.uk/news/uknews/1559594/Church-to-tackle-shortage-of-vicars.html

## THE GENERATIONAL CRISIS

A third crisis is less visible to churches but more profound. This is the mass exodus of a whole generation of Christians from the institutional churches. In *You Lost Me*, David Kinnaman of the Barna group charts that a significant number of young people in their twenties and early thirties, sometimes called the millennial generation, have left the church of their youth. Though active in the church as teenagers, the majority of them drop out.[23] In an earlier book *unChristian*, Kinnaman discusses what a new generation of "outsiders," those who have not been in church, really think about Christianity. He says:

The title of this book, *unChristian*, reflects outsiders' most common reaction to the faith; they think Christians no longer represent what Jesus had in mind, that Christianity in our society is not what he meant it to be.[24]

Of millennials, only two out of ten believe that church attendance is important. More than one third of millennials (35 percent) take an anti-church stance. Fifty-nine percent of millennials who grew up in church have dropped out at some point. More than one half of millennials have not been to church in at least six months.[25] The Census Bureau projects that this millennial generation has surpassed the baby boomer generation and has become the largest generation in America.[26]

---

23. David Kinnaman, *You Lost Me: Why Young Christians are Leaving the Church . . . and Rethinking Faith* (Grand Rapids, MI: Baker Books, 2011), 1–30 *passim*.

24. David Kinnaman with Gabe Lyons, *unChristian: What a New Generation Really Thinks about Christianity* (Grand Rapids, MI: Baker Books, 2007), 15.

25. "Americans Divided on the Importance of Church," Barna, 24 March, 2014. https://www.barna.com/research/americans-divided-on-the-importance-of-church/

26. "Millennials Overtake Baby Boomers as America's Largest Generation," Pew Research Center, 25 April, 2016. http://www.pewresearch.org/fact-tank/2016/04/25/millennials-overtake-baby-boomers/ (accessed 15 May, 2017).

While *The Ministry of Expansion: The Priesthood of the Laity* does not speak directly to this crisis, it opens the door for a variety of creative approaches in ministry to this growing, disaffected group. One such pattern is that of a house church ministry carried out in conjunction with a larger "mega church." Already many evangelical churches are using this methodology with great success.

However, an even more far-reaching house church movement, which sees the church in small gatherings as the "primary" form of the church, is underway across the world. In 2009, Christian leaders from forty nations met in New Delhi, India to report and explore the scope and significance of house-based communities. It was reported that in many nations sizeable house church movements have emerged. One estimate was that the number of house churches in Europe have already reached or surpassed ten thousand. Australia could have up to ten thousand and New Zealand, six thousand.[27] In America, the Barna research group reports:

> Today, house churches are moving from the appraisal phase into the acceptance phase. We anticipate house church attendance during any given week to double in the coming decade, and a growing proportion of house church attenders to adopt the house church as their primary faith community. That continued growth and public awareness will firmly establish the house church as a significant means of faith experience and expression among Americans.[28]

---

27. "Simple Church Europe," http://www.simplechurch.eu/articles/full/house-churchmovement-seems-unstoppable/ (accessed 24 April, 2015).

28. "House Church Involvement is Growing," Barna, 19 June, 2006. http://www.simplechurch.eu/articles/full/house-churchmovement-seems-unstoppable/

It remains to be seen whether the millennial generation and those that follow will find in small communities, centered around the Eucharist, a fitting expression of their faith and spur to social involvement. This may have the potential to reach those who have pursued their spiritual quest through greater sensitivities to the environment as well as those seeking greater economic justice and non-violent solutions to conflicts in the world. If such a simple church can be maintained despite diverse schedules and the attraction of other interests, lay presidency of the Eucharist can provide local leadership at little or no cost.

Whether or not small Christian communities will expand among millennials, some young people may find spiritual strength from their families gathered about the Eucharist. Allen's argument in both *The Ministry of Expansion* and *The Family Rite* is that the family again becomes the center of the Christian church and its ministry. Church-going families have long realized that church activities often have had the effect of dividing families as the church sought to minister to various age and interest groups. Allen's insights as well as the ancient Hebrew custom of a home-based Sabbath rite might interest those who continue in the faith without a church affiliation. Centered about the Eucharist at a special family meal, discussions about the purpose of life, the meaning of death, and many ethical issues faced by various members of the family might encourage both a vibrant family life and a meaningful faith.

## THE ECCLESIASTICAL CRISIS

*The Ministry of Expansion* also addresses a fourth crisis. This might be called the "ecclesiastical" crisis. Though lay people easily move between denominations and among congregations, their clergy are usually locked into structures from which there is no escape. Clergy find that their salaries, their retirement, their hopes for promotion or a call to another congregation depend on how they respond to the next denominational crisis. When there is an honest debate about worship, church involvement in national politics, clergy's sexual preferences, or questions of biblical interpretation, the issues often become political as various sides fight to gain control of the denomination and force others to accept their position.

Now, nearly every denomination is wracked by divisions and threats of schism. Few lay people are involved in such conflicts because they have long enjoyed the freedom to accept or reject the teaching of church authorities especially on controversial matters. Because their income and future do not depend on the outcome of these quarrels, they may be inclined to be more objective in the debates and more loving to their opponents.

Should some of these same lay people be called upon to preach, teach, and preside at the Eucharist, one might see many of these denominational conflicts subside. Since their position is neither dependent upon a denominational party or seminary, they are most likely to represent the convictions of their congregation. Since few, if any, would aspire to leadership positions within the church body, personal ambition would not likely be a motivation for continuing conflict.

Such lay leadership within congregations might also serve to heal some of the divisions of Christ's church. Despite the ecumenical progress made in the last century with the World Missionary Conference, the World Council of Churches, the World Conference on Evangelism, and many inter-denominational discussions, many congregations from different denominations at the local level are still badly divided. When warned by denominational officials to watch out for the false teachings of another church, a lay minister once said, "If they only let us alone, I think we could solve the differences between these two churches." Were the leadership of more congregations made up of such lay people, we might find that congregations might better share the richness of their own traditions and receive the blessings of others.

There was a revival of interest in the insights of Roland Allen in the early 1960s. The new nations of the world were reclaiming their own heritage and independence. Like the sun, colonialism was setting in the west. Allen had long claimed that many native people in missionary lands had resisted the Christian message not because of its content but because of the imperial practices of the western churches exercised through seminary-trained clergy. If Allen's proposals were adopted, perhaps there might be another "spontaneous expansion of the church" across the world.

In Africa, China, India, and Latin America, this is indeed what has happened, not because of a change in mission policies but because the new wine of the gospel could not be contained in the old wineskins. Independent native Christian leaders, referred to by Allen in chapter three in *The Ministry of Expansion*, simply carried out the mission. Using a wide variety of worship forms suited to their cultures, they sang their faith into the hearts of their neighbors. In the West, however, the home of the settled churches, Allen's proposals were largely ignored. Perhaps the reason was best given by Sir Kenneth Grubb when he wrote that while Allen spoke of how to start from the beginning, he was less clear on how to start halfway down the course. For Grubb and most mission thinkers change was possible in missionary lands but not at home, where the church and her policies were long established.

However, at the beginning of a new century the chief challenges to the church are not in missionary lands; they are within the Western churches. Many denominations are aging and losing members; they also are rent by controversy. Rather than representing the ideal of a single apostolic ministry groomed by Christ, professionally-trained and paid clergy are most often responsible for continuing divisions. The most rancorous debates in the church are about such clergy, their education, their upkeep, their gender, their sexual preferences, and even their sexual activities. With the vigorous debates about these professional clergy now paralyzing the very life of most denominations, will Christ's people be able to meet the various crises they face at the beginning of a new century?

In *The Ministry of Expansion*, Allen argues that lay people be encouraged to celebrate the sacraments so that any small group of Christians can be completely supplied with all it needs to survive and grow as the church. Here he is careful to stress that he is speaking chiefly for those without benefit of clergy. Yet, once Christians realize that God has given the sacraments to the whole church and that each group of Christians can choose who should preside at the Eucharist and baptism, a marvelous transformation is in the offing. Now a lack of funds need not limit the church from expansion; the ministry of peers can make the church more relevant in a time of cultural diversity. Old wounds between Christians can be healed; together they can aid the world's unfortunate. Though long viewed as a radical voice in missionary circles, Roland Allen's chief contribution to the twenty-first century may be that he speaks a word of hope. If any group of Christians can be fully the church, no power on earth can prevail against it. Instead such a church can become the leaven in every society, and all of Christ's people can be empowered to serve.

# BACKGROUND AND OVERVIEW OF *THE MINISTRY OF EXPANSION*
Steven Richard Rutt

Two of Roland Allen's early publications titled *Foundation Principles of Foreign Missions* (1910)[1] and *Pentecost and the World: The Revelation of the Holy Spirit in "The Acts of the Apostles"* (1917)[2] disclosed his ongoing focus of the Holy Spirit's ministry within the early church. After much reflection on the Apostle Paul's missionary journeys and epistles to the churches, Allen came to the conclusion that both pneumatology and ecclesiology—*Spirit* and *Order*—were essential to understanding Paul's missiology. On the one hand, Allen's devotion to Pauline *pneumatology* emphasized the importance of spiritual gifts (1 Cor 12–14), while, on the other hand, he recognized that the Spirit's empowerment for the mission of the church actually worked within the context of *ecclesiological order*: "Let all things be done decently and in order" (1 Cor 14:40). Allen found in Paul's missionary theology a symphonic blend of pneumatology (Spirit) and ecclesiology (Order), and this theology became the basis for Allen's missionary principles and practices.

Later in life Allen wrote two other significant works which reflected his missiology of "Spirit and Order." First, while in his early sixties, he wrote, *The Ministry of Expansion: The Priesthood*

---

1. Roland Allen's first edition was titled *Foundation Principles of Foreign Missions* (Bungay, Suffolk: Richard Clay & Sons, 1910) the reprint was titled *Essential Missionary Principles* (Cambridge: Lutterworth, 1913), to be followed by another reprint titled *Missionary Principles—and Practice* (2006).

2. Roland Allen, *Pentecost and the World: The Revelation of the Holy Spirit in "The Acts of the Apostles"* (London: Oxford University Press, 1917).

*of the Laity* which advanced a theology of the sovereign work of the Holy Spirit within indigenous churches, as the "direct internal impulse of the Spirit"[3] (Acts 8:14–17). As a high church Anglican, he maintained that bishops were consecrated to oversee the planting of churches. And yet, it became evident to him that within many frontier regions where no ordained ministers existed (especially, within African and Asian contexts) that the Holy Spirit sovereignly created new churches through the ministry of the laity. This reminded him of the early church's expansion in pioneer regions and suggested: "Spirit *before* Order." On the one hand, this phenomenon disclosed the inevitability for the existence of independent churches. On the other hand, in his attempt to preserve what he believed were principles which undergirded apostolic order—bishops ordaining the laity for service under apostolic succession—he proposed a *well-ordered* ecclesiology which argued for "Spirit *with* Order."

Second, as Allen's missiology developed over time, he recognized the need to capture the essence of the laity's significance in church growth where *every Christian is a missionary*, and therefore, at the age of seventy-five, wrote *The Family Rite*.[4] This work advocated the planting of churches in remote areas even when ordained clergy were not present to lead, since, as he argued, it was still necessary to provide a faith community where there would be the frequent practice of the Lord's Table for the church's spiritual health. His decision to refer to this as a family rite was rooted in his understanding of the Passover observance (Ex 12).[5]

---

3. See chapter 3, page 91.

4. This work was never published during Allen's lifetime. David M. Paton later published it. See "The Family Rite" in David M. Paton, ed., *Reform of the Ministry: A Study in the Work of Roland Allen (London: Lutterworth Press, 1968)*, 189–219.

5. Roland Allen, *The Family Rite*, 6–7. Unpublished manuscript.

## WHAT ABOUT APOSTOLIC SUCCESSION?[6]

Before closely examining *The Ministry of Expansion* it is necessary to address the overarching influence of *apostolic succession* and how this relates to Allen's thought. The ongoing conversation of apostolic succession continues to remain an ecclesiastical topic within the context of the established church today. Some contemporary evidence of this is disclosed through the writings of Edward Schillebeeckx, a Roman Catholic theologian, who indicated a radical break from a *mechanical* belief in apostolic succession.[7] As a leading theologian within Roman Catholicism since Vatican II, his challenge to the traditional position on apostolic succession reasserts the necessity for further discussion within the Church of Rome.

The same can be said of the Anglican Church's *mechanical* practice, as Allen argued in *The Ministry of Expansion*. He recognized the differences of opinion about ecclesiastical government within his own Anglican Communion during the nineteenth century among high, low, and broad churchmen, as well as between liberals and evangelicals. Allen's ecclesiology, shaped by the high churchmen of the Oxford Movement, did maintain an episcopal order of apostolic succession with a specialized priesthood. Yet, certain voices such as Samuel Coleridge and Thomas Arnold (broad churchmen), argued for the universal priesthood of the laity for the Church of England.[8] This issue was addressed by Allen within *The Ministry of Expansion*.

---

6. Allen, *The Ministry of Expansion*, chapters 2–3. See also, Arthur W. Haddan, *Apostolical Succession in the Church of England* (London, Oxford and Cambridge: Rivingtons, 1879), 1–2.

7. Edward Schillebeeckx, *Ministry: A Case for Change* (London: SCM Press, 1984) and Schillebeeckx, *The Church with a Human Face: A New and Expanded Theology of Ministry* (London: SCM Press, 1985).

8. Allen C. Guelzo, *For the Union of Evangelical Christendom: The Irony of the Reformed Episcopalians* (University Park, Pennsylvania: The Pennsylvania State University Press, 1994), 117.

The Anglo-Catholic emphasis of the Oxford Movement articulated especially through the writings of Bishop Charles Gore and Professor Robert Campbell Moberly argued for a more disciplined approach to church order, and yet, apparently did not consider how this could be applied to pioneer regions where the Anglican Church had been spreading within British colonialism. This seemingly neglected application was confronted by Allen. In order to address this issue, he developed a systematic rationale within *The Ministry of Expansion*[9] which, on the one hand, did *not* argue against the validity of apostolic succession, as presented by Gore and Moberly, but, on the other hand, did challenge their legal, formal, and strained theory, which he believed, resulted in an exclusiveness that denied any lay expression of sacramental grace and advocated a "teaching which strangles us."[10]

In 1889, Charles Gore (consecrated bishop in 1902) wrote an apologia concerning what he believed was "the principle of the apostolic succession" in his book *The Ministry of the Christian Church*.[11] Then, in 1897, Robert Moberly wrote *Ministerial Priesthood*, essentially as a study of the Anglican Ordinal.[12] Allen believed these books did not specifically address the spontaneous growth of the church, which was occurring in the non-Western world (Africa, Asia, and Latin America) without the presence of episcopally ordained clergymen. He thought Gore and Moberly were out-of-touch with the expansion of the church outside of the Western context. Referring to these writings, Allen noted:

> These books have now long been the standard works for many theological students: therefore,

---

9. See chapter 7
10. See preface.
11. Charles Gore, *The Ministry of the Christian Church* (London: Rivingtons, 1889), v.
12. Robert Campbell Moberly, *Ministerial Priesthood* (London: John Murray, 1897).

I have restricted myself almost entirely to them. In so doing I recognize sadly that I must appear to careful readers, and to all careless ones, to be opposing those good and eminent men. That is most unfortunate. . . . I would gladly have avoided it, but I am compelled to run that risk because of the widespread influence which they exercise, and the fact that appeal is so often made to them by the men who teach what I maintain to be false. I am compelled to do it because, if I had not mentioned them, I should have seemed to be ignoring the most powerful objections to the practice which I advocate.[13]

Allen attempted to contextualize some apostolic principles to what he observed were neglected regions of the world that lacked episcopal response, and this compelled him to argue against their theory of apostolic succession. For Allen, apostolic succession exists not to sideline the ministry in some sort of ecclesiastical castle but to proactively advance the apostolic faith and reproduce apostolic churches.

## CONVICTIONS ON COMMUNION

In terms of *lay presidency* at the Lord's Table, what did Allen believe? First, according to Hubert Allen, his ecumenical-style of ministry never diminished his devotion to Anglican High Churchmanship.[14] Second, concerning Allen's tenacious persona when he addressed various institutional deficiencies and unreasoned practices in the church, he took a *radical* position.[15]

---

13. See preface, page 72.
14. Hubert Allen articulated how his grandfather remained faithful to a High Anglican belief in the centrality of the Eucharistic Sacrament; Interview with Hubert Allen on 18 October 2010.
15. Interview with Hubert Allen on 18 October 2010.

Allen believed in the appropriate administration of Holy Communion by ordained priests and bishops. In pioneer regions where properly ordained clergy were *not* locally present, he believed that Anglican order still necessitated the continuance of the sacramental meal whenever Christians met together.[16]

Who, therefore, was qualified to administer Holy Communion if ordained clergymen were absent? Allen came to the conclusion that the church must act for herself since, if Christ is spiritually present in the Holy Communion, "it is Christ who consecrates the elements Himself, and that He will not desert them because they have no ordained priest at hand."[17] He believed there was sufficient ground to justify such an action, as recorded in the New Testament among the young churches of Samaria, Lydda, Joppa, Phoenicia, Cyprus, Antioch, Galatia, and Rome.[18]

## PREFACE TO *THE MINISTRY OF EXPANSION*

In the preface to *The Ministry of Expansion*, Allen initiates the conversation by confronting a certain "cruel bondage," which he believed hindered churches from receiving the sacramental grace due to non-existent ordained clergy within their context. His passion comes through clearly on this matter within the opening paragraphs with phrases such as, "I see Christians scattered as sheep having no shepherd. . . . I feel compassion. . . . And I write as one of them. . . . I speak of *our* fears . . . *our* hesitations . . . *our* common condition."[19] He then calls upon the bishops to solve the current deficiency.

First, Anglican order necessitates a basic assumption that Christ's sacraments are for all his children and that it is unnatural to deny sacramental grace to anyone. Second, he argued that

---

16. See Matthew 18:20; 1 Corinthians 11:17–34.
17. See chapter 1, page 79.
18. See chapter 4.
19. See preface, page 71.

there is a proclivity in human nature to create customs and traditions which ultimately disallow basic principles. However, when the basic principles of sacramental grace are freely administered, whether clergy are present or not, this grace will generate life.[20] Third, the deficiency of any proactive approach from the bishops at the Lambeth Conference, as stated in their Report (1930) to address with compassion and strategy the current crisis of "hundreds of thousands"[21] of communicants without any resident priests to administer the sacraments, was considered unacceptable according to his analysis. Fourth, his assessment of the crisis did *not* suggest that he ruled out the necessity to maintain Anglican order through the significance of episcopal ordination. Allen believed the bishops needed to demonstrate a preemptive approach to the crisis by offering to ordain indigenous leadership wherever a community of Christians gather for worship.[22] Fifth, the non-existent priests and bishops exclude nothing, therefore, he believed, this vacancy made room for Christians to act sacramentally for themselves.

Allen believed that the indigenous church ought to be empowered—from the beginning—to administrate its own activities. This was foremost in his thought: "I should like to see it accepted as a general principle that converts should be presented by members of the church to the church, and accepted by the church and baptized on the authority of the whole local church acting as a church."[23] The possibility to engage the laity to take ownership of its local activities stemmed from his apostolic missionary ecclesiology which sought to empower the members to act for themselves when necessary.

---

20. See chapter 1.
21. See chapter 1, page 78.
22. See chapter 1.
23. Roland Allen, *Missionary Methods: St. Pauls or Ours?* (Cambridge: The Lutterworth Press, 1912, 2006), 99.

## FUNDAMENTAL PRINCIPLES

An overview of Allen's first chapter disclosed three significant points: 1) that Christ ordained His sacraments for *all* His children, 2) that Christ's command to observe the sacrament of the Lord's Table regularly applies to all, and 3) that it is unnatural to deny this sacramental grace of Communion even when an ordained minister is not present to preside. After many years of firsthand missionary experience, especially within countries where British colonialism had extended its borders, Allen observed how many colonialists (members of the Church of England) were living within regions without any Anglican priests and, therefore, were deprived of the sacraments. Since the ecclesiological practice within the Church of England necessitates the frequent practice of the Lord's Table by duly ordained priests, Allen came to the conclusion that whenever Anglicans relocated to regions where priests were not present, he proposed the following: "faithful Christians must obey Christ as well as they can, assured that it is Christ who consecrates the elements Himself, and that He will not desert them because they have no ordained priest at hand."[24] Allen argued that in this case, Christ's command trumps ecclesial custom and, in order to reinforce this point, quoted Jesus' words: "Where two or three are gathered together in my name there am I in the midst of them" (Matt 18:20).[25] This pastoral concern for the spiritual health of fellow Anglicans compelled Allen to address this deprivation of the Lord's Table as "worse than unnatural,"[26] for, in his opinion, it advanced a "custom . . . tradition . . . theory" at the expense of the command "to receive the grace which Christ offered" in the Holy Communion.[27]

---

24. See chapter 1, pages 79.
25. See chapter 1, page 81.
26. Ibid.
27. See chapter 1, page 77.

It is important to point out *again* that Allen's position was not an argument against the Anglican order of apostolic succession but against the exclusiveness that denied any lay expression of sacramental grace and which advocated a "teaching which strangles us."[28] On the one hand, his pneumatology of "Spirit *before* Order" was highlighted within the conclusion of this chapter when he proposed:

> I am certain that they [Anglicans without any resident priests] would find grace to help in time of need [Heb 4:16]. "O taste and see how gracious the Lord is" [Ps 34:8]. . . . Christ gave us the sacraments. Taste and see. If a priest appears occasionally, receive him: but in his absence act for yourselves.[29]

On the other hand, his ecclesiology of "Spirit *with* Order" within this chapter "did not argue that episcopal ordination was of no importance,"[30] but rather that it was a "divine order [that] is for building up, not for destruction: it is to maintain the sacraments of Christ, not to annul them; it is to establish the Church, not to hinder its establishment."[31] Allen's ecclesiological argument affirmed the *normal* "Order" of Anglican clergy (ordained by bishops) administering the Lord's Table. He also affirmed a *flexible* "Order" for the laity to administer the Lord's Table in given situations where clergy were not present upon the belief that "it is Christ who consecrates the elements Himself."[32]

---

28. See preface, page 72.
29. See chapter 1, page 81.
30. See chapter 1, page 80.
31. See chapter 1, page 81.
32. See chapter 1, page 79.

## HABIT AND TRADITION

The second chapter of Allen's work began with the recognition of how unreasoned habits within the established Church of England quite often neglected to consider a place of ministry for the laity. Fixed patterns of practice within the Church of England remained as habits and traditions not to be reformed. Allen examined "our hesitation to minister for ourselves" as that which stemmed from custom, not as that rooted through any reasoned conviction.[33] Then, he drew attention to Anglican mission expansion, wherein "we went abroad and found ourselves where there was no priest at all."[34] His perception of minimal visionary thinking on the part of English bishops to address the problem was only indicative of a systemic failure.

He argued that throughout history the English Church had learned to adapt to its growing challenges by appointing indigenous leadership whenever and wherever it was necessary. Consider his comments, in another publication, concerning the growth of the indigenous Church of England in the sixth century when Pope Gregory the Great sent Augustine and his associates as missionaries to England:

> If we examine Bishop Stubb's *Registrum Sacrum Anglicanum*, we find that the last of the Augustinian mission to be consecrated was Honorius (AD 627) to Canterbury. In that year Felix, a Burgundian, was consecrated to Dunwich. After that the only foreign bishops were Theodore of Tarsus (AD 668) to Canterbury, Agilbert (AD 650) to Dorchester, and Leutherius (AD 670) to Winchester . . . If we look at the sees established—Lichfield was founded in AD 656, and

---

33. See chapter 2, page 83.
34. Ibid.

all the names of its bishops are native; Lindsey was founded in AD 678, and the names of all its bishops are native; at Dunwich, after Felix the Burgundian, all the names are native; at Elmham (AD 673–AD 1055) they are all native; at Worcester (AD 680–1095) they are all native; at Hereford (AD 676–1079) they are all native. In fact, see after see was established, and see after see was established with a native bishop.[35]

Allen's forthright appeal to the historic English Church's ability to adjust to current needs (seventh to eleventh centuries) is an example of how he reasoned when dealing with contemporary challenges. And yet, what was the Church of England to do after it had extended its influence through colonial control in distant lands without enough trained clergy to meet the immediate needs? The answer to this question is found in chapter three which advances the apostolic principle of training home-grown leadership.

## CHARISMATIC MINISTRY

In the third chapter, Allen addressed his readers with the assumption that they were familiar with the ministry about which he was writing. He reminded them that this type of minister already appears within their missions overseas and serves spontaneously, without ordination, and was unable to be classified. They tended to be out of place within the existing mission structures. Allen argued that this ministry did not oppose church order. He pointed to the New Testament for support, though contemporary writers excluded such ministry.

---

35. David M. Paton, ed., *The Ministry of the Spirit: Selected Writings of Roland Allen* (Grand Rapids, MI: William B. Eerdmans, 1960), 179, as cited from the chapter entitled "Domination" in Allen's *The Case for Voluntary Clergy* (1930).

Some clarity and definition is in order when attempting to understand Allen's use of the words *charismatic, charis,* and *charisma*. Lesslie Newbigin properly identified that "Allen was not a prototype of the contemporary evangelical charismatic—much as I think he would have welcomed the charismatic explosion."[36] First, Newbigin's accurate analysis of Allen's thinking is disclosed in the Spirit emphasis that is rooted in his ecclesiology as "the Pentecostal gift."[37] However, this does not imply that he was a charismatic in the sense of the modern understanding of speaking in tongues; neither does it suggest that he was opposed to this grace (*charis*). Instead he emphasized, in a primary sense, *charismatic ministry* for the equipping of the church through "that direct internal impulse of the Spirit"[38] and also, in a secondary sense, for the church's empowerment from "a spiritual illumination"[39] through the gifts of the Spirit (*charismata*).

Second, his use of the word *charismatic* ought to be understood as an extension of his belief in the abiding validity of apostles, prophets, and teachers—"wandering evangelists," as he called them—who demonstrated significant trans-local ministry "ascension" gifts (Eph 4:8). Allen recognized both the significance of the church's applied *charisma*—as a gift of grace—within the ordination rite. The person called in ministry accepted both the *charisma* from the church's rite (laying on of hands for ordination) and commission to officially serve, in addition to the individual *charisma* given by the Holy Spirit.

In terms of the *charisma* which was evident among those not ordained by the church, he cited both Sundar Singh of India and

---

36. See Bishop Lesslie Newbigin's analysis in the foreword of Hubert J. B. Allen's *Roland Allen: Pioneer, Priest, and Prophet* (Cincinnati, OH: Forward Movement Publications; Grand Rapids, MI: William B. Eerdmans, 1995), xiii–xv.
37. Allen, *Pentecost and the World*, 11.
38. See chapter 3, page 91.
39. Allen, *Pentecost and the World*, 46.

the "Prophet Harris" of West Africa.[40] Singh and Harris were indicative of a plethora of ministers with *charisma* who functioned outside the context of the established church. Allen stated that

> they are men whom missionary teachers would deem ill-qualified for the work . . . No one sends them out to do it . . . they work outside all ecclesiastical organization, independent of all ecclesiastical authority and supervision . . . with no recognition, no commission, no ordination . . . but are moved solely by an internal impulse . . . yet they certainly perform a ministry . . . in the eyes of those among whom they work.[41]

Allen recognized these unique expressions of *charisma* at work in what he would call the apostolic method. He was not alone in thinking this way about Harris. Lamin Sanneh, almost eighty years after Harris' death in 1929, speaks of Harris' ministry.[42] Harris encouraged thousands of Christian converts (French Government officials calculated about 100,000 converts)[43] to receive instruction within both Protestant and Roman Catholic communions.[44] Both Allen and Sanneh recognized that Harris had this type *of charisma*, even though he was not commissioned by any ecclesiastical body.

Allen believed the Pauline emphasis on leadership gifting[45] provided a contextual setting to argue for historic "apostolic" ministry once again, as evidenced by those first "wandering

---

40. This evangelist's name is William Wade Harris.
41. See chapter 3, pages 92–94.
42. Lamin Sanneh, *Disciples of All Nations: Pillars of World Christianity* (Oxford: Oxford University Press, 2008), 201.
43. Sanneh cites William J. Platt, *From Fetish to Faith: The Growth of the Church in West Africa* (London: Cargate, 1935), 87.
44. Sanneh, *Disciples of All Nations*, 195.
45. Ephesians 4:11 is cited in chapter 3, page 95.

evangelists and prophets"—not known by the established order of apostles—which had established communities throughout Antioch, Lydda, and Rome. Within the context of leadership gifting he pointed out that these functions of prophets, evangelists, pastors, and teachers actually "follow apostles in a list of the gifts."[46]

When applying apostles to his early twentieth century context what did he mean? Allen believed these apostles—"wandering evangelists"—were the gifted missionaries who planted and equipped the churches. They were the "itinerant" missionaries who were known to work outside of the established order, yet could function within the established structure wherever and whenever resident elected leadership (i.e., bishops, deacons) accepted their vocation. For Allen, this was apostolic order. Even Moberly recognized that "Apostles no doubt would be thought of as characteristically non-local."[47] This apostolic work is an extension of the apostolate, which is how Allen understood this itinerant ministry.

For example, Allen wrote a bishop of Central Tanganyika: "In a diocese like yours, surely you are in the position rather of an apostle than of a territorial bishop."[48] This emphasis of apostolic principles and ministry was paramount in Allen's missionary ecclesiology. At the end of chapter three in *The Ministry of Expansion*, he concluded with a brief story from Mildred Cable's book *Through Jade Gate* telling how a missionary teacher was invited to the Chinese district of Kansu to instruct various people in the Bible and "not only baptized his converts but taught them all to observe the Lord's Supper."[49]

---

46. See chapter 3, page 95; See also, Ephesians 4:11; 1 Corinthians 12:28.

47. See chapter 3, page 98; Moberly, *Ministerial Priesthood*, 163–64.

48. Allen's letter to the Bishop of Central Tanganyika, USPG X622, Box 6, letter 137A, June 10, 1930, Oxford, Bodleian Library.

49. See chapter 3, page 99. See also Mildred Cable and Francesca French, *Through Jade Gate and Central Asia: An Account of Journeys in Kansu, Turkestan and the Gobi Desert* (London: Constable & Co., 1927).

## THE PRACTICE IN THE EARLY CHURCH

Allen began chapter four by examining the New Testament, drawing attention to the churches of Samaria, Antioch, Cyprus, Lydda, Phoenicia, Joppa, Galatia, and Rome. Moving beyond the Scriptures, he then drew attention to the non-canonical *Didache* where it seemed to show no evidence that the Eucharistic officers were even "ecclesiastically ordained." By appealing firstly to the Didache and then to evidence given by Tertullian, he attempted to find evidence that, in even in the absence of a priest, Christians still celebrated the Lord's Supper. He then critiqued Bishop Gore's repudiation of the evidence put forth by Tertullian. Allen was convinced there was sufficient evidence in the early church for what he was suggesting to be applied to his situation.

From this chapter the reader gets a glimpse of Allen's commitment to the *primacy* of Scripture when defining apostolic ministry and his willingness to cite early church *tradition* by appealing to the *Didache*.[50] Allen made use of *reason* to argue from Scripture and tradition when applying his interpretation of these "evangelists called Apostles, Prophets, and Teachers, who wander about, and Churches established by them whose local officers are called bishops and deacons and are elected."[51] He clearly distinguished between itinerate apostolic order (i.e., apostles, prophets, teachers) and the resident local ministry (i.e., bishops, deacons) from what he believed was the *Didache's* application of apostolic instruction.[52] The *Didache* referred to the Eucharistic meal (14:1–3) as a common expression of the faith with the understanding that

---

50. J. B. Lightfoot and J. R. Harmer, "The Didache or The Teaching of the Twelve Apostles" in *The Apostolic Fathers*, 2nd edition, edited and revised by Michael W. Holmes (Grand Rapids: Baker Book House, 1989), 149–58.

51. See chapter 4, page 104.

52. Thomas O'Loughlin, *The Didache: A Window on the Earliest Christians* (London: SPCK, 2010), 168–70.

not all of these primitive churches had resident clergy, as seen in the instruction to give "the first fruits" (i.e., the tithe) to the poor "if you have no prophet [settled in your community]" (13:3). This reference to a "prophet" who might settle within a certain community implied their vocation to be itinerant in nature. This point is critical within Allen's understanding of the vocation of itinerant evangelists.

## WE CANNOT GO BACK

In chapter five, Allen parsed some of Moberly's comments and "abstractions" (*Ministerial Priesthood*, 109–10) that tended to disparage the newer churches (younger churches) that were "springing up," many of which were *independent* of the "organized" church.[53] Allen argued that the newer churches within pioneer regions were experiencing challenges very similar to that which the early Christians experienced, such as being "remote from the ecclesiastical authorities."[54] Allen was not arguing "against an ordained ministry" rather he defended the legitimacy of these newer "churches [that] were springing up" outside the influence of the organized church.[55] The fact that the laity were already managing these developing churches, he argued, seemed to be "in open defiance of [the] authority" of the organized church.[56]

Allen went on to argue against what he thought was an improper use of the word "covenant" in that Bishop Gore and Dr. Moberly—as well as their followers—promoted the "legal, formal, strained" *interpretation* of apostolic succession, that being, the ecclesial custom that denied the laity any authorization to administer the sacraments. His missiology argued for a return to

---

53. Allen's original edition of *The Ministry of Expansion* referred to these newer churches as "infantine." However, for the sake of clarity, these churches will be referred to as "newer" churches.

54. See chapter 5, page 111.

55. See chapter 5, page 113–14.

56. See chapter 5, page 117.

an apostolic understanding: "the promise is not without the Covenant, but within it."[57] And, any custom and habit that denies the laity to administer the sacraments when clergy are not physically present is a misapplication of what "the Covenant of promise" means under the definition of "the Gospel" (Gal 3:1–9).[58] Those who disagreed with Allen's return to the early church's practice of lay presidency (in given circumstances) argued that such a return was not progress but reverting backwards. Allen insisted that it was "not backward for us" to return to *apostolic precedent* because "we are back in their day" with the same spiritual needs.[59]

## THE PRIESTHOOD OF THE LAITY

Allen wrote in chapter six that the ministers who celebrate the Eucharist are doing this "not vicariously for the congregation, but representatively, and that it is the whole body which offers" the sacrifices of praise and thanksgiving.[60] Gore and Moberly's "logical conclusion" was, in his opinion, false, as it would "make the sacraments entirely depend upon the will of a bishop."[61] The belief that this "doctrine as set out by these theologians [asserted that] none of us are empowered to act [implies that] Christ's sacraments are annulled for us," and, this, he believed, was against the apostolic teaching concerning "the universal common priesthood of Christians."[62] He then cited Bishop Lightfoot who argued:

> It may be a general rule [but] an emergency may arise when the spirit and not the letter must decide . . . [that] the higher ordinance of

---

57. See chapter 5, page 119.
58. See chapter 5, pages 118.
59. See chapter 5, page 111.
60. See chapter 6, page 121.
61. See chapter 6, pages 123–24.
62. See chapter 6, pages 124, 126.

>the universal priesthood will overrule all special limitations . . . [and the] layman will assume functions which are otherwise restricted to the ordained minister.[63]

Bishop Lightfoot's recognition of "an emergency [that] may arise" for sacramental administration *by the laity*, is contrasted with Moberly's and Gore's interpretation.[64] This clearly demonstrated how Allen advanced the apostolic faith's Trinitarian understanding of the church's one and the many—individual (Christian) and group (church)—where the Christian "is a member of a priestly body and shares all the powers of the body, the universal being in the particular because the Spirit is one in the universal and in the particular."[65]

The law of the universal priesthood of the church, Allen believed, could not be understood as a separate law of episcopal ordination. Both are united together, he argued, and "are not two laws, but one [that is] a gospel law," which, according to Bishop Lightfoot, "opens to us the door of grace."[66] This understanding related to the legitimacy of lay presidency for administering sacraments in "emergency" situations, as Lightfoot argued. Allen concluded this chapter by empathizing with the "men who are beyond the reach of ordination or whose ordination may be hindered by a tradition not less legal and cruel than this."[67]

---

63. See chapter 6, page 128. See J. B. Lightfoot, *Commentary on Philippians: The Christian Ministry* (London, 1868), 268.
64. See chapter 6, page 128.
65. See chapter 6, pages 129.
66. See chapter 6, page 130.
67. See chapter 6, page 132.

## PRESUMPTION

Allen begins his final chapter by making a distinction between "settled churches and [those] outside them" and then unpacks the significance of "that ministry of expansion" which has its stimulus from "the charismatic ministry."[68] Here he specifically states the centrality of his missiology—the Holy Spirit's sovereignty over church expansion. Some "felt that it would be *an act of presumption to dare* to hold a service of any kind" without the presence of regularly ordained ministers.[69] Allen disagreed on the grounds that whenever the Holy Spirit empowers the laity "to observe His Last Supper" it is *not* a presumptuous act, and therefore, is "it not then greater presumption to disobey Him than to obey Him?"[70] Next, he argues for the early church's practice where "dioceses were small, and the bishop was the representative of a Christian community which knew him, and which he knew personally."[71] A restoration of this practice, he believed, would solve the problem.

Allen argued that within Anglican missionary methods, a new problem had developed where vast diocese "leave large numbers of groups without any ordained priests" and subsequently, in order to solve this problem, imposed a European model of theological education upon indigenous candidates seeking ordination. This, he argued, placed too much credence on "the act of an individual [priest]" rather than "the act of a Church which meets to perform its own proper rite."[72] This shift, he argued, looked "not at the group but at individuals" and presented "a great gulf between the priest and the Church."[73] This gets at the heart of Allen's ecclesiology which argued for candidates to be trained locally and *not*

---

68. See chapter 7, pages 134–36.
69. See chapter 7, page 137.
70. See chapter 7, page 138.
71. See chapter 7, page 139.
72. See chapter 7, pages 140.
73. Ibid.

to be sent to a theological seminary elsewhere. He believed the diocesan bishop exemplified true apostolic order when he trained candidates for ordination.

Consequently, Allen reiterated the purpose for his apologia by reemphasizing that "this book ought properly to be addressed," *not* for those within the existing and settled churches, but rather for those who are "geographically beyond the reach of any bishop [and] outside the boundary of the organized Church."[74] Allen recognized that those denominations "who utterly reject the doctrine of Apostolic Succession"[75] still tend to restrict lay presidency, as soon as they become highly organized and practice the system of "ordained stipendiary ministry."[76] He concluded this "little book" by reaffirming reverence to the Anglican order of episcopacy and "the relationship which should exist between the ministry of expansion and the settled ministry."[77] His apologia for *the ministry of expansion* was rooted in the charismatic dynamic that works within and extends from the *priesthood of the laity*. Hence, in many respects Allen can be considered a pioneer in modern missiology.

## CONCLUSION

My research concluded that Allen's argument for apostolic mission—as disclosed in *The Ministry of Expansion*—stemmed from an integrated pneumatology (Spirit) and ecclesiology (Order) that was shaped by the Apostle Paul's missionary principles, methods, and practices. Although Allen conventionally maintained his belief in apostolic succession and high church episcopacy for the planting of indigenous churches, it became evident that his understanding of the Holy Spirit's empowerment

---

74. See chapter 7, pages 141.
75. See chapter 7, page 142.
76. Ibid.
77. See chapter 7, pages 141, 144.

of the laity actually proposed the prioritization of "Spirit *before* Order." This produced, on the one hand, the inevitability for the existence of independent churches and on the other hand, in an attempt to preserve what Allen believed were principles that undergirded apostolic order, a challenge for bishops to proactively advance the *apostolic order* by ordaining the laity who were already serving these younger churches.

Allen's observations of this *charismatic* dynamic of the church's expansion within the non-Western world compelled him to argue on behalf of these "younger" or "newer" churches. He defended the legitimacy of these newer churches that were emerging outside the influence of the organized church—Spirit *before* Order—where *the priesthood of the laity* faithfully served these communities of faith. As a missionary analyst, he interpreted his context as similar to the early stages of the younger churches of Samaria, Lydda, Joppa, Phoenicia, Cyprus, Antioch, Galatia, and Rome. Throughout Allen's missionary journeys and itinerant ministry, he affirmed the sovereign acts of the Holy Spirit that were at work within these younger churches. And, it is this pastoral concern that provided the impetus for him to write *The Ministry of Expansion*.

Allen's emphasis on a return to the early church's practice of lay presidency (in given circumstances), he believed, was a return to *apostolic precedent*. His defense for sacramental ministry in the newly formed churches actually created a context for a *well-ordered* ecclesiology to eventually emerge, that being, "Spirit *with* Order." We saw that as an Anglican clergyman and missionary, Allen had reverence for divine order. Disclosed within the context of this unpublished work he clearly distinguished between itinerate *apostolic order* (i.e., apostles, prophets, teachers) and the resident local ministry (i.e., bishops, deacons) from what he believed was primarily inspired within the Bible, and, secondarily, outlined within the early church's application of apostolic instruction as revealed in the *Didache*. In the final analysis of *The Ministry of*

*Expansion*, it is important to disclose that Roland Allen's missiology actually proposes a "Spirit-*inspired* ecclesiology" designed to accommodate the *charismatic* dynamic in order to equip, commission, send, and expand the church throughout the world.

# PART II
## ROLAND ALLEN'S
# THE MINISTRY OF EXPANSION
## THE PRIESTHOOD OF THE LAITY

Editorial Note: We have attempted to preserve Roland Allen's work as it appeared in the original and have only made minor editorial changes and the occasional bracketed insertion in cases where clarity would otherwise be significantly impaired. One example of this editorial liberty was in the removal of chapter summaries that preceded each chapter in Allen's work. These "analysis" pages, as he described them, were collections of fragmented sentences, lists, and statements only understood if read in the chapter's context. In no instance were Allen's arguments and conclusions modified or altered.

The two typed manuscripts of Allen's work at The Bodleian Library of the University of Oxford have some variations between them. Many of these are related to proofreading marks and handwritten statements found on the manuscripts. One sizable discrepancy, for example, is that most of chapters two and four are missing from one of the typed manuscripts. When it was not clear as to which of the two manuscripts were supposed to be the final version, we have provided footnotes with commentary.

Finally, Roland Allen did not always provide the complete publication information when citing sources in this work. There are several instances in which Allen was citing from Charles Gore's *The Church and the Ministry* but the page numbers matched instead with Charles Gore's *The Ministry of the Christian Church*. We were able to locate these particular quotes (word-for-word, or very nearly) in both sources—we think perhaps that *The Church and the Ministry* might have been a new and revised version of *The Ministry of the Christian Church*, published thirty years later. Because Roland Allen's citations were unclear, we have cited the source that best corresponds with what Allen had written and the page numbers that he provided.

# PREFACE

This little book is not a theoretical treatise on the Ministry; it is an attempt to show a way of release to men and women who are bound in a cruel bondage, and hindered by it from stretching out their hands to receive what Christ Himself offers to them.

Not only are they themselves starved, but the expansion and growth of the Church is checked, because it is by their fullness of life that the whole Body should advance. Christians without Sacraments lose not only grace for their own lives as individuals, but lose also the corporate life, the manifestation of the Body to which others who are seeking the way of Christ can attach themselves. They suffer, and with them the whole world suffers. There is stagnation where there might be fullness of life and growth in Christ. As I look out over the world I see Christians scattered as sheep having no shepherd, where I might see small Churches springing up and increasing in number, filling the whole world with joy and gladness. I feel compassion. I feel compassion; and, because I feel compassion, I put myself into the place of these scattered sheep, and I write as one of them. I write to real men and women, some of whom I know in the flesh. I write to them as one of them. I speak of *our* fears, of *our* hesitations, of *our* common condition.[1] I address them directly, "I" speak to "you."[2] I might have put these few chapters into the form of personal letters.

Because I am writing not a theoretical treatise on the ministry, I have referred to very few books. It is to Bishop Gore's

---

1. Emphasis in the original.
2. Quotes in the original.

*The Church and the Ministry* and to Dr. Moberly's *Ministerial Priesthood* that appeal is most often made by those who most narrowly assert the teaching which strangles us. These books have now long been the standard works for many theological students: therefore, I have restricted myself almost entirely to them. In so doing I recognize sadly that I must appear to careful readers, and to all careless ones, to be opposing those good and eminent men. That is most unfortunate. Again and again, I repeat that I do not believe that the doctrine to be found in their books can properly be applied to us, but I cannot disguise from myself the fact that by constantly referring to these two books I must appear to be singling them out for attack.

That I regret most sincerely. I would gladly have avoided it, but I am compelled to run that risk because of the widespread influence which they exercise, and the fact that appeal is so often made to them by the men who teach what I maintain to be false. I am compelled to do it because, if I had not mentioned them, I should have seemed to be ignoring the most powerful objections to the practice which I advocate.

I say that I do not believe that the language of these great masters can properly be applied to us, and I attack that application. I wish that I could write so as to make it perfectly clear that within their own limits I accept their teaching as sincerely as I revere their persons. But I cannot even do that. Their theory of the Apostolic Succession appears to me legal, formal, strained, and based upon extremely doubtful interpretations both of the language of the New Testament, and of the passage from the early Church Fathers which they quote. They fail to convince me even within their limits. That cannot but appear in my language, and I am sorry for that; because here I am not arguing against their theory of Apostolic Succession. If I were doing that I would have written a much larger book, and a very different one. All that I am arguing here is that, whatever view we may take of their writings, it need not, ought not, to hinder us. Consequently, I bitterly regret being compelled to write what I know will be interpreted as an attack on their position, and I feel it all the more because I do not hold their position. All that I can do is to beg any who may read what I have written to be assured that I have tried my utmost to avoid such an attack. I am not discussing their doctrine; I am simply discussing what I believe to be a false application of it, and nothing more.

If my ordination empowers me to minister, it does not follow that my ordination excludes the ministry of others.[3] I can believe the positive without asserting the negative. I cannot believe that others who obey the Lord's commands to observe His Sacraments are doing wrong because they have not my orders. Such a statement seems to me wholly opposed to the spirit and teaching of Christ. He, in His love, provided for His children means of grace, and who am I to deny them on the ground that I have been ordained and they have not? If I could believe that the Sacraments of Christ were not for men cut off from the ministrations of the episcopally ordained either by distance or by a cruel tradition, I could believe that Sacraments were not for anyone anywhere. I would rather be a Quaker than admit that Sacramental grace was given to me to hinder others from grace. If assertion of my own ordination involved the deprivation of others, I would rather deny my own ordination. To claim grace for myself in such terms as to

---

3. In the two typed manuscripts of *The Ministry of Expansion*, this paragraph begins with the following sentence: "I am a priest, and I know that grace is given in ordination for the work of the ministry; but I am equally assured that the grace is positive, not negative." However, in one of those copies, it appears that Allen made an editorial mark to remove most of this sentence (which appears at the bottom of the typed page). However, the three words, "positive, not negative," appear at the top of the subsequent page and lack editorial markings for their removal. Because they do not comprise a complete sentence and lack editorial marks, I have included the full sentence in this footnote.

exclude others from grace is to me utterly wicked, a very denial of Christ. But I am certain that no such claim is required of me.

If it is not, it is high time that all who know that it is not should speak out and teach diligently and constantly that it is not; for nearly all of our people have a sort of vague idea that it is. If that were not so, I should have no occasion to write this little book. All would know that when they, or others near them, were in need and no ordained priest was at hand, it was their duty to administer the Sacraments. All who desired the Sacraments might then enjoy them, and receive the grace of them. Little groups of Christians all over the world might organize themselves to live a godly and a Christian life bound together by the observance of the rites which Christ ordained to unite and support them in His service. A habit, long established, would have to be broken; but some would begin to break it, and all would feel, what they do not feel now, freedom to break it. They do not feel that freedom now, because they are taught directly in so many words by some of the clergy, and tacitly and by implication by all, that to break that habit would be wrong. That is why I have written.

# CHAPTER I
# THE FUNDAMENTAL PRINCIPLES

Some years ago I received a letter from a correspondent in India who told me that he had spent much of his life in places where there was no resident "padre" and that he had asked a member of a religious community what he should do to maintain his religious life. The advice given to him was that, since he was cut off from actual participation of the Sacrament, he should practice Spiritual Communion. He told me that he had done that for many years, and twice he sent me little services of Spiritual Communion which he had himself prepared; but he said, "The clergy do not easily understand the difficulty of that practice; and Christ our Lord, knowing the weakness of our nature, provided for us the sacrament to help us, and I long for the sacrament."

That letter made me think. I began to wonder whether Christ in ordaining His sacraments for us intended us to be deprived of them when we most feel the need of them. The cleric whom my friend consulted took it for granted that if a priest were not at hand to minister the sacrament there could be no sacrament; but is that what Christ intended? I came to the conclusion that it was not.

(1) It is impossible for me here to argue that Christ in ordaining His Supper as a memorial of His death was ordaining a rite for all His children to observe. The Catechism teaches us that there are two sacraments "generally necessary" to salvation, and I accept that as sufficient. If any one questions whether Christ did ordain those sacraments for all His children let him read no further; for this little book is not written for him.

(2) If it is admitted that Christ directed His servants, generally, to observe His sacraments, if that teaching which we commonly hear at home, that partaking of the Holy Communion as an act of obedience to Christ is true teaching, then anything whatsoever which prevents men from observing it is something which overthrows and annuls the command of Christ for them. I say that no custom or tradition can annul a command of Christ for Christians. For them, His command must be supreme. Only another direction of Christ Himself could suffice for us. Only if He, as explicitly as He directed us to observe His Last Supper, directed us that under certain conditions we were not to do so, should we be justified in setting the command aside. I beg you consider that carefully, for we shall certainly find no command of Christ, as explicit as His command to observe His sacrament, directing us when, and under what circumstances, we are not to observe it, other than His teaching of the moral and spiritual conditions which exclude us from forgiveness of sin such as Pharisaism which asks no forgiveness, or a spirit which refuses forgiveness to others, and the like.

That is the foundation on which I build. I put the command of Christ first and foremost and above all else. If He commands, we must obey. Our Church and our Bible alike assure us that He did command, and that He commanded us, each one of us, who hear His word. Then nothing can annul that command. If anyone does not accept that, let him read no further. This little book is not for him.

(3) If it is true that obedience to Christ and observance of His sacraments has been a means of grace to us. If in drawing near to Christ in His appointed way, we have found help in time of need, and a strong salvation, and a sure hope; if in offering the sacrifice of praise and thanksgiving we have ascended into the heavenlies and have tasted of the powers of the world to come, then I aver that any argument which would deny us that grace must be nothing short of a direct command from heaven, if it is to hinder us with any show of reason.

That, I suppose, is what Bishop Palmer meant when he wrote the other day, "It is worse than unnatural to suppose that God thinks of any Church rule as so much more important than the Eucharist itself, that people who for no fault of their own were without a priest must also be without a Eucharist."[4] It is true that Bishop Palmer was not thinking of us when he wrote that sentence; but the expression certainly applies to us. We are precisely in the position which he describes, and his conclusion holds for us. It is most unnatural; it is worse than unnatural; it is wicked. If anyone does not accept that, let him read no further; for this little book is not for him.

Now there is a theory prevalent in the Church today, there is a tradition commonly supposed to be almost divine, there is a custom firmly established, which denies all those truths which I have just enunciated. That custom, that tradition, that theory prevented my friend from stretching out his hand to receive the grace which Christ offered to him, and compelled the cleric whom he consulted to advise him to practice spiritual communion in lieu of the sacrament which Christ ordained.

It seems to me a very strange thing that men who have devoted themselves to the religious life, who have undergone a long and careful training in prayer and meditation, men who before all others should be most capable of spiritual communion, lay such stress upon frequent celebrations of the sacrament of Holy Communion for themselves, that they think it is a great hardship to be deprived of the sacrament for a short time, and yet advise a layman who has none of their advantages to try to satisfy himself without the sacrament. It is like a channel swimmer in the face of a torrent into which he would not venture without a lifebelt advising a schoolboy to swim without one. We see religious communities in which Holy Communion is celebrated every day surrounded

---

4. E. J. Palmer, "The Proposed Union of Churches in South India," *The Church Quarterly Review* 110 (July 1930), 248.

by groups of Christians for whom a celebration is a comparatively rare event, once a month, once a quarter, or even less frequently than that. If these religious men with all their training need frequent celebrations, how can they expect men who have had none of their advantages to grow and prosper in the religious life unless the sacraments are always at hand for them in time of need. I once asked a sister in a community whether she thought it right that a priest should be kept to celebrate for her community when Christians all around her were starving. I said, "If once a quarter is sufficient for them surely once a quarter ought to suffice for you. Would it not be better that your priest should go away to minister to them more often, and appear here just so often, and no more often, than he can visit the others? She answered me, "I too have often thought that." But you observe that the authorities of these communities insist upon frequent celebrations for their own communities. They know the need. And, in truth, the communities should not have less than they need; but the Christian folk scattered round them should not have less than they need.

The cases of deprivation are very numerous. I know that numbers have nothing to do with the principle, that one case is sufficient to cry for a remedy, and that multiplication of it by tens of thousands does not affect the principle; but I know also that we are influenced by numbers, and that a fault multiplied ten thousand fold impresses us more than the fault in a single case, though a single case ought to suffice. It seems worse to us in the case of ten thousand than in the case of one. For that reason I wonder that the bishops who assembled at Lambeth were not staggered by the Report of their Committee on "The Ministry of the Church." "Hundreds of thousands," it was said in that Report, "of Christians of our own and other races are living, and, as things are at present, must continue to live almost entirely cut off from the ministry of the sacraments." That such a Report could be written by Christian bishops and accepted without protest by a still larger number of Christian bishops, without one word of compassion or of penitence, is amazing and appalling. Christ, it is written, had compassion on the multitude because they were as sheep having no shepherd, but our bishops see the multitude scattered without a shepherd and utter no sigh of pity, no word of shame. "We are taught," they say, "that only a priest can consecrate the elements," and thereafter they discuss the possibility of ordaining voluntary priests in a few cases and shut their eyes to the vision of the multitude scattered and destitute.

We cannot but observe the form of that expression in the Report, "we are taught." That expression is not equivalent to "we teach": it is not equivalent to "we know" or "we are persuaded," or even to "we believe." No one who was stating a truth which he held strongly and firmly could express it in the form of these bishops. "We are taught" does not imply acceptance; it may even imply doubt. They are not agreed on the matter, they do not accept the doctrine as certain divine truth, and consequently they naturally use a formula which hesitates between acceptance and refusal and can be adopted equally by those who believe it and those who do not.

Their action corresponds to this form of expression. They do not go to their people and say plainly, "Without our ordination you must not obey Christ"; neither do they say, "When you are beyond our ministrations you may, and you ought to, act for yourselves." They do not preach plainly, "None but an ordained priest can consecrate the elements under any circumstances, anywhere," neither do they teach plainly, "In the absence of an ordained ministry faithful Christians must obey Christ as well as they can, assured that it is Christ who consecrates the elements Himself, and that He will not desert them because they have no ordained priest at hand." They simply let things slide, sending ordained clergy where they can, and leaving the rest to find out the way for themselves, if they can.

In *The Case for Voluntary Clergy*, I argued that if bishops teach that the sacraments are generally necessary to salvation and believe that they are set over the flock of Christ to ordain clergy to minister the sacraments, they are committing a great sin against Christ when they put congregations of Christians in the care of lay readers and catechists and leave groups of Christians without any ordained clergy resident among them, unless, at the very least, they offer to ordain; but now I am considering what laymen ought to do when they are left destitute, either because the bishop does not even know of their existence, or because he is too far away to care for them, or because he admits himself powerless to help them.

I have known in my life a man cut off, as my friend in India was cut off, from the regular ministrations of ordained clergy who celebrated himself with his family. I once asked a bishop whether that man did right, but the bishop gave no answer. In this little book I argue that he did his duty and did it rightly.

In *The Case for Voluntary Clergy* I did not argue that episcopal ordination was of no importance; neither am I now going to argue that it is of no importance. I am going to argue that that teaching that only a priest can consecrate the elements, when it is applied where there is no priest, when it is used to annul the commands of Christ, is false. I am going to argue that *the non-existent can exclude nothing*, and that Christian men ought to obey Christ and to seek His grace in His sacraments regardless of a non-existent priest. For people in our position, bishop and priest are non-existent. When we need the sacraments of Christ they simply *are not there*. That is the fact with which we are face-to-face. We cannot choose. We must either act for ourselves or disobey Christ; and as I began, so I end; that is not a choice about which a Christian ought to have any doubt. That teaching of which the bishops spoke, however true it may be in organized Churches where an ordained ministry exists, becomes an utterly impossible teaching for us for whom the ordained ministry is non-existent.

When a Christian is alone, he is alone with Christ. There is no one to dispute his acts. If he celebrates for himself alone, he does so because he believes that Christ told him to "do this in remembrance of me," and that Christ will receive and bless him if he does it. Who dare say Christ will not? Where there are three, they agree that one of their number shall act for them on this occasion. They approach Christ together and seek His grace. Can any man say that Christ will deny it, because none of them has been ordained? That were to admit what we have agreed to be "worse than unnatural." There is here no denial of any theory of ministry in established Churches, there is no schism, there is no presumptuous claim to a priesthood which we do not possess. We simply do what Christ told us to do as we can, not as we can not. That is all.

I wish that all our people would learn that lesson. I am certain that they would find grace to help in time of need. "O taste and see how gracious the Lord is." No Church Historian can rob men of Christ's gifts if they draw nigh to Him humbly and do what He told them to do. No Church ordinance, if there really is such an ordinance, can rob them by overruling Christ. Christ gave us the sacraments. Taste and see. If a priest appears occasionally, receive him, but in his absence act for yourselves. If he is not there, he is not there. He might as well be at the ends of the earth as far as you are concerned. Where bishops cannot, or will not, act, there no law of episcopal ordination can run. A divine order is for building up, not for destruction: it is to maintain the sacraments of Christ, not to annul them; it is to establish the Church, not to hinder its establishment. A blind acceptance of a teaching that only a priest can consecrate the elements, applying that teaching to men who have no ordained priest, is pure negation. It is death. It leaves us hopeless, and helpless, when we need the sacraments of Christ. The Gospel is not negation and death.

Let us flee from anything "worse than unnatural"; and turn to Christ Who said, "Where two or three are gathered together in my name there am I in the midst of them." That is not negation and death, but life. Let us take Christ at His word, and then we cannot go wrong.

# CHAPTER 2
# HABIT AND TRADITION

The first point that I want to make clear is that our hesitation to minister for ourselves is rooted not in any reasoned conviction but in custom and habit which we have never questioned nor examined.

At home in England we lived in a society where the ministrations of ordained clergy were always at hand. It never entered our heads to enquire whether under any circumstances a layman might minister; because the presence of the clergy rendered the question superfluous.

We knew quite well that in the Prayer Book certain acts were reserved to the priest, and that if a deacon took a service he omitted the absolution. We knew that no deacon could celebrate the Holy Communion. That sufficed. There was obviously an order of clergy to whom it appertained to celebrate the Holy Communion. That sufficed.

Then we went abroad and found ourselves where there was no priest at all, or else possibly one came round at more or less uncertain intervals and held a service which we might attend; but in the intervals between his visits there was no Church. We missed the sacraments; but we took abroad with us the ideas and the habits established at home, and it never occurred to us that we were deprived without good reason. We took it for granted that what a layman could not do at home, he could not do abroad. We took it for granted that it could not be right for him. We took it for granted that it had been proved by someone at some time that it was inevitable, just as the loss of the amenities of home life and the society of friends and relations was inevitable. We accepted the position without dispute, and most of us still so accept it.

Our acceptance is supported by the attitude of the clergy. They too think in that way. They come out of the same surroundings, they have imbibed the same traditional habit of thought; and they are never in our position. They are never cut off as we are; because being in the class which traditionally can minister the sacraments, they can never be deprived of them. They have been taught that it is their part to minister sacraments, the part of the laity to accept their ministrations, and they never think outside that teaching. Consequently their teaching, so far as they teach at all on this subject, is always within the limits of their presence, and in terms decided by their presence. They cannot even conceive a layman ministering except as infringing their prerogative. Bishops and priests alike take the same attitude. They all speak as if they were always present, and never direct men what to do when they are absent.

If we would see how much more we are restrained by habit than by reasoned conviction, we have only to begin to enquire into the argument upon which the tradition stands.

Apart from the inherent impossibility of its truth as applied to us, of which I spoke in the last chapter, the moment that we open any book by any great Church historian on the subject of the Ministry of the Church, we are face-to-face with the fact that there is no agreement between scholars on any theory which would exclude us. Let us suppose for the moment that the theory of the Apostolic Succession maintained by scholars like Bishop Gore and Dr. Moberly would exclude us, (though I shall prove in a moment that it is not addressed to us), in opposition to it are other views upheld by men like Bishop Lightfoot and Dr. Hort and Dr. Sanday which certainly open wide the door for us. It is impossible then for anyone to say that the tradition is proved, if by proved he means demonstrated to the satisfaction of all reasonable men. The most that could possibly be said for it would be that it is agreeable to teaching of some scholars. But this is a very different thing from taking it for granted that it has been proved that such action as I am advocating is wrong.

Most of the people who, in the absence of a priest, hesitate to act for themselves, have not accepted the teaching which might seem to exclude us: not even all our bishops and priests have accepted it. Then hesitation to act cannot possibly rest upon a theory which has not been accepted. In earlier days in our colonies scarcely any of the Christians who went abroad had ever heard of that theory, except perhaps as a theory held by some other Christian body, and if they had been asked whether they believed it, they would have unhesitatingly answered, No. Yet they did not act for themselves. Why? Not because their inactivity rested upon reasoned conviction that the action would be wrong, but simply because they had been in the habit of thinking so, in circumstances where there was no need for them to act on their own behalf. Their ideas did not rest upon an intelligent conviction, but upon an unreasoned, unexamined habit.

But, it may be said, that unreasoned habit was right and now the reasons for it have been thought out, and made explicit. I have already pointed out that the theory so explicitly stated is not a demonstrated truth, but only the theory of a certain number of scholars who are opposed by others who dispute their conclusions. But we must go further than that: We must observe that the theory which seems to exclude us is argued by men who are not considering our case. Our case is far from their thoughts. It would be a totally different matter if scholars like Bishop Gore and Dr. Moberly had written deliberately and definitely in opposition to the practice which I am suggesting. Then anyone who advocated what I advocate might well be asked to meet them on their own ground and to answer their argument. It would be hard indeed for a poor scholar like me to enter upon a dispute with such great doctors of the law. I suppose that I should have to appeal to the other great doctors—the Horts, the Sandays, the Lightfoots—and to shelter myself behind them. It is true that they are no more thinking of our case than the others, but at least their writings give us hope where the others appear to close the door against us; and I might appeal to them. But that is quite unnecessary, because I might agree with Bishop Gore and Dr. Moberly and yet advocate the course which I am advocating, for their arguments are not addressed to me.

How entirely they are thinking far away from us we shall see at every step, but it may be well to illustrate it here. Dr. Moberly and Bishop Gore speak always as if there was a choice between the ministrations of an episcopally ordained clergy or some other before their readers. For us there is no such choice. The choice for us is between the ministration of a layman or none at all. There is no choice. Either a layman takes the service or no religious service is held. Dr. Moberly and Bishop Gore speak always as if the performance by a layman of any rite or function which normally at home belongs to the commission of a bishop or of a priest was a desertion of the true order, a rejection of the ministry of the clergy, an infringement of their rights, an assumption of their powers; but we know perfectly well that in our case there is no assumption of their powers nor any infringement of their rights. We do not assume that we are clergy, we do not pretend to any clerical rights, we do not desert any one; for there is no one to desert. Bishop Gore and Dr. Moberly are always thinking in terms of a settled organized Church with its ministers ordained in due succession, and all the passages which they quote from ancient authors and Church Fathers about the position of the bishop or his presbyters speak in terms of Churches in which bishops and presbyters resided. In such cases for a layman to officiate was certainly to forsake his bishop and to act in his despite; but in our case neither bishop nor his clergy are anywhere near us.

Again, Dr. Moberly in answering the question, *How can you tell whether there was or was not a link missing in the chain, somewhere perhaps in the thirteenth—or the third—century?* uses this argument:

> Those who speak lightly of what may have happened long ago, are they indifferent to the things

which concern themselves? Would they accept as their bishop one who was consecrated to episcopate by laymen? or receive absolution in their hour of anguish, or the eucharistic gifts in their highest worship, from one who had received his ordination at the hands only of the unordained?[5]

The question so presented could only arise in Churches where a regular order of ministers was normal. With us, the question is not whether we would receive absolution and the Eucharistic gifts in our hour of anguish at the hands of a man who was ordained by unordained men, but whether we would receive them at the hands of men who claimed no ordination or not at all. And I say that many of us would gladly do so. If a good godly layman whom we knew well, whose life and piety claimed our respect, celebrated for us in our hour of anguish, we should receive with joy and much comfort. Wouldn't you? I am certain that I should. I might indeed shrink from a man who claimed to have been ordained when I was sure that he had not, but from a good Church layman who claimed no powers of the sort? I ask, would not you accept his ministrations? I certainly would. I do not believe that there is one of our bishops who would excommunicate either him or me for doing it.

I remember Bishop Palmer at a meeting stating the case of three officers in the trenches during the war. One celebrated for the others. Bishop Palmer said that he had consulted a learned Canonist and that the answer given to him was that that was a valid rite. Whether it was valid or not does not seem to me a question which I should ever ask. It was a pious act and one befitting Christian men. Would you ever question it? Would you question whether Christ would accept them? The answer that we give in that case, is the answer which we give in our own. But, it may be

---

5. R. C. Moberly, *Ministerial Priesthood* (London: John Murray, 1907), 123–24.

said, we are not in imminent peril of death. We are: who knows that we are not? But we are not cut off as they were from the regular service administered by the ordained cleric? We are. The plain fact is that we are living and thus without any properly organized Church. That a cleric may be able to pay us a visit from time to time does not alter that fact. As Bishop Gore told us, "The primary importance of the church's organization is that it is local."[6] And we have no local Church organization.[7]

That Dr. Moberly puts the case as he does proves at once that he is not thinking, any more than Bishop Gore was thinking, of men in our case, but of men living in a society in which ordained ministers are at hand. It is, then, most unreasonable to apply their teaching to circumstances which were not in their thoughts when they wrote. We need not decide the questions in dispute between the great scholars. None of them are considering our case or arguing on that plane. It makes no difference whether we accept the argument on the one side or on the other, or whether we leave such disputes as beyond our province to be settled by the learned. We can go our way assured that none of their arguments touch us because they apply only to regularly organized Churches. Within that limit they are no doubt important, but outside it they have no more weight than arguments concerning the legal position of

---

6. Charles Gore, *The Church and the Ministry* (London: Longmans, Green and Co., 1919), 49. This quote is found as a handwritten editorial mark in Allen's manuscript and contains minor inaccuracies. The actual Gore quote is: "The primary importance of its organization is *local*."

7. These last four sentences of the above paragraph were later handwritten additions by a proofreader in only one of the two originally typed manuscripts. The original concluding statement in that paragraph was also removed from that manuscript. However, in both manuscripts the following statement concluded the paragraph before the later four sentences were added: "So far as the bishop and his clergy are concerned they might as well be at the North Pole, for all the help that they can give us at this moment."

Justices of the Peace in England would have for a colony of castaways on a Pacific Island.

We see then that the restraint of ministrations under our circumstances is not based upon reasoned conviction but simply upon habit and a tradition which ought never to have been carried outside the sphere in which it grew up.

But to reform an established habit which has become instinctive is a far more difficult matter than to correct a false opinion which rests upon argument. Where it is recognized that the opinion rests upon an argument, an argument can be applied directly to refute it, and if the argument which refutes it is accepted, the opinion is abandoned. But in the case of a habit which rests not upon reasoned conviction but upon feeling and sentiment and cherished associations, no argument by itself touches the source. All that the argument can do is to release a pent up internal discontent with the habit, by showing that the arguments on which it is supposed to rest are empty of force. Then the internal discontent will break through the habit, and men pluck up courage to cast it off.

When then I now proceed to show how vain are the restraints in which we have hitherto imagined that we were held, I am appealing to the longing which abides in the hearts of Christian men to obey Christ and to enjoy His grace in the sacraments which He ordained for them. I am really all the time seeking not so much to convince their minds that a restraint is unreasonable, as to release their souls from bondage, by showing them an open door in Christ.

# CHAPTER 3
# CHARISMATIC MINISTRY

By "charismatic ministry" I mean here a ministry which is exercised by a man who is moved to perform it by an inward, internal impulse of that Holy Spirit who desires and strives after the salvation of men in Christ. I do not deny that men receive a charism, a gift of grace, for their ministry in ordination; but I use the word "charismatic" to express the ministry which is exercised in virtue of that direct internal impulse of the Spirit, as distinguished from the ministry which is exercised by those who have been ecclesiastically ordained or commissioned. That use of the term "charismatic ministry" is very familiar; and it is reasonable, because it expresses the fundamental character of the ministry of which we speak. It expresses its distinctive character; and we ought no more be robbed of its use in that distinctive sense by the argument that all ecclesiastical ministry is fundamentally charismatic than we ought to be robbed of the term "voluntary clergy" to distinguish clergy who serve without any fee or stipend from "stipendiary clergy," by the argument that all stipendiary clergy are voluntary because none of them is compelled to serve against his will.

In this sense, then, of the term "charismatic ministry," we are all familiar with a "charismatic ministry" today. We know that scattered all over the world there are men who exercise a ministry wholly outside the organized ministry of the Church, far beyond the reach of the bishop who represents to us Church order, simply because they are moved by the Spirit.

We all hear of them, but few of us see them. Their work is generally discovered by missionaries who hear of them, either because they, or their converts, appeal for further instruction, or because rumor gets abroad and a missionary goes to inquire of their truth. Thus we read of them in missionary magazines, or hear of them in countries which we may visit, just as we hear or read of some natural curiosity in the country. I have heard of them wherever I have been, in China, India, or Africa, and I have read of others in other parts of the world. I suppose no one can live long in any country where Christian communities are surrounded by great numbers of non-Christians without at least hearing a rumor of one, unless he lives wholly apart from the society of the native Christian community, outside the world in which such reports are handed on. No one can read missionary magazines and not hear of them from time to time; for some of them attain widespread fame, like prophet Harris, whose work on the Ivory Coast and the Gold Coast (Ghana) was widely advertised a year or two ago by the agents of the Methodist Missionary Society, or Sundar Singh, who was brought to Europe from India and spoke and wrote so that his name became very widely known.

These are the exceptional cases: behind them are many others whose fame never extends beyond their own country, or province, or district; and behind them again is a still larger number whose influence does not reach outside their own village, or town, or its immediate neighborhood. We know that they exist, but we do not know their numbers, still less the names of more than a few of them. From time to time we are told that the majority of the converts in some area are the fruit of the labor of these men, but their names are unknown and unrecorded.

These men appear often in the most unexpected places and at the most unexpected times. No man can foretell when or where they will appear. No man can—no man does—discover them before they begin their work, no man chooses them and trains them deliberately for the work which they perform. Often they are men whom missionary teachers would deem ill-qualified for the work which they perform. Often they are men who, when they first met missionary teachers, were passed by as of no remarkable power. They were hidden; then they appeared: they are not discovered until they have done their work.

They do their work spontaneously. No one sends them out to do it, no one appoints their place or time; they work outside all ecclesiastical organization, independent of all ecclesiastical organization, independent of all ecclesiastical authority and supervision—most of them unknown to any ecclesiastical authority. Some of them like Sundar Singh went out of missionary training schools unsatisfied and unregarded, with no recognition, no commission, no ordination; some of them have received no more than the simple instruction given to catechumens. They are not sent out by authority to work but are moved solely by an internal impulse.

They seldom seem able to do their best work within the organization of a Mission. Sometimes one is caught and drawn into the organization of a mission to work under the direction of authority in the class of paid evangelists; but only too often he seems to lose some of his power when he works under those conditions. \*\*At the moment when the missionary, or the bishop, first discovers his work and takes it under his own direction and wins the man to become one of his evangelists or teachers, he speaks as if he had gained a great addition to his evangelistic force; but curiously little is said of him after a few years. Commission by authority does not seem to make him more effective as an evangelist; payment of a salary does not seem to add to his spiritual power; the organization of the mission does not seem to be his spiritual home.\*\*[8]

---

8. These sentences appear here in both of the original typed manuscripts. In both documents, these pages contain proofreader's markings. However, one of the manuscripts has a single diagonal line draw through it while the other document does not. My assumption is that this is a mark to delete the paragraph. With editorial markings on both pages, however, I am not

These men cannot be classed. They are called, or call themselves, by many titles—evangelist, or teacher, being apparently the most common—where any title at all is used; but they cannot be placed in the class of Evangelists, or in the class of Teachers, as those terms are applied to mission workers. Some of them do works of healing by prayer which occasionally attract the attention of doctors, and are sometimes considered miracles by others, but these works of healing are generally alluded to only incidentally in some account of their work which reaches a foreigner, and we cannot class those who perform them as healers. No distinct title can be given which would include them all; they certainly do not belong to any definite order in the Church; yet they certainly perform a ministry; they certainly are ministers of Christ, in the eyes of those among whom they work.

Similarly among our own race overseas there are men who perform a charismatic ministry. Far away from all organized Church life, in the sense in which organized Church life depends upon a ministry regularly ordained by a bishop, they gather their families and their friends and neighbors together and conduct religious services. From time to time we read of them in missionary magazines, or in accounts of the early struggles of settlers overseas, but not all who do this work are known or mentioned. Many of whom we hear nothing are doing that work today. They too perform a ministry, they too are ministers of Christ to those whom they help; but they, like the others, are exercising their ministry, undirected, uncommissioned, unordained by any ecclesiastical authority.

This ministry is not opposed to Church order. These men are not deserting their bishop, nor creating a schism, nor seeking to set up a new organization over against the Church: they are doing

---

certain whether or not the diagonal line was drawn prematurely or later added to note the removal of the paragraph. The two documents do not include any dates as to the timing of the editorial markings. At other times it is clear, in both documents, when passages are to be removed.

a work upon which the regular organization of the Church can be established just as soon as that organization can be properly applied. Often the bishops and clergy first hear of their existence because they [these unordained men] desire Church order. Then the difficulty arises that the bishop, who today rules over a vast diocese which nominally includes them, can do nothing for them. He sends a catechist or a lay teacher, or appoints a lay reader as if that was Church order. They ask for Church order and they are given by the man set to represent Church order, something that is not Church order: they ask for bread and are given a stone.

Now the language used in the New Testament presents no difficulty; it rather suggests that this kind of ministry was quite familiar to the Church of the apostolic age. There we read that "they that were scattered abroad went everywhere preaching the word" (Acts 8:4);[9] or that ministry and teaching and ruling are gifts of the Spirit in the same order as liberality and mercy (Romans 8:6–8); or that prophets and evangelists, pastors and teachers follow apostles in a list of the gifts which Christ gave to His Church (Ephesians 4:11). When we read of wandering evangelists whom the Christians are urged to assist on their way; when we read of communities of Christians at Antioch, Lydda, and Rome which have sprung up we know not how; when we read of Christians in the neighborhood of Colossae who had never seen the face of St. Paul—we naturally conclude that a ministry familiar to us today was at work then; and we naturally imagine that if one of these modern unordained evangelists and pastors and teachers could be carried back to that age, he would find himself quite at home, and that the Apostle St. Paul would look upon him as nothing unusual or strange. There is no word in the New Testament to suggest that his ministry was not a ministry quite familiar to that age.

---

9. Quoted from KJV.

But when we turn to the pages of Bishop Gore or of Dr. Moberly we find expressions which would rather seem to suggest that this exercise of such a ministry is not compatible with the principle of order in the Church. The expressions used by them are so unlike the expressions of the New Testament that, whereas the expressions of the New Testament are quite agreeable to it, the expressions used by these writers would seem formally to exclude it.

Bishop Gore, for instance, uses an expression like this: "An authoritative Mission is indeed essential for all evangelistic work, for 'how shall men preach except they are sent?'—how, that is, can anyone take upon himself so responsible an office?"[10] And he suggests that even St. Paul did not exercise his office without a commission from the Church, for he speaks of the laying on of hands by the prophets and teachers at Antioch mentioned in Acts 13:3 as a proof that later prophets and evangelists must have been ecclesiastically ordained, saying,

> the evidence of the Acts as to the laying-on of hands, which gave, or confirmed, the mission even of St. Paul and St. Barnabas, will not allow us to suppose that the inspiration of these later prophets would have enabled them to dispense with ecclesiastical ordination by apostles or apostolic men.[11]

Similarly Dr. Moberly says,

> Any aspiration to ministry in Christ's church, or attempt to discharge its duties, however otherwise well-intentioned, would be a daring presumption at the first, and in practice a disastrous weakness, in proportion as it was lacking in

---

10. Charles Gore, *The Church and the Ministry*, 234.
11. Charles Gore, *The Ministry of the Christian Church* 2nd ed. (Waterloo: Rivingtons, 1889), 285.

adequate ground to believe in its own definitely, validly, divinely received authority to minister;[12]

and he makes it quite clear that in his view nothing but episcopal commission can give that assurance. He too appeals to the case of St. Paul, saying,

> the principle that commission to ministry is by laying on of hands . . . is no where made quite so emphatic as when St. Paul, with Barnabas—after his Divine call, his mission to the Gentiles and his courageous preaching, and with all his sense of vocation to apostleship direct from Jesus Christ personally—yet with fasting and prayer, is set apart by the laying on of hands of his brother 'prophets,' for the great missionary work to which the Holy Ghost was calling him;[13]

and later in his book discussing Ephesians 4 he speaks of evangelists thus:

> "Evangelists" is no doubt a missionary term; and it is obvious that in the condition of Christianity in the time of St. Paul, the missionary officers were in no sense less important than the officers of settled communities. We may fairly assume that any duly authorized missionary ministers who were not apostles might be called evangelists. . . . It would be the simplest of suppositions to suppose that if a presbyter from any city became a missionary, he would, *qua* missionary, be called "evangelist"; while evangelist would be the most direct and natural term for those who would have

---

12. Moberly, *Ministerial Priesthood*, 102.
13. Ibid., 108.

been presbyters if their work had been (as it was not) in a settled community. To find therefore 'evangelists' thus mentioned, and to find them, at such a date, inserted in mention between apostles and presbyters would be perfectly natural. Apostles no doubt would be thought of as characteristically non-local. That their non-local subordinates should be named with them (whether constituting an Order or not) before the local officers of communities would in itself raise no difficulty or question at all.[14]

Here it is plain that Dr. Moberly pictures the evangelists of the New Testament as in the position of those evangelists who in our Missions are employed under the direction of the bishop; and he thinks that simpler and more reasonable than to think of them as in the position of those men of whom we have been speaking. But is it possible to imagine that men like those whose work I have described did not exist in the apostolic age? I find that quite impossible, and consequently I find Dr. Moberly's "simplest of suppositions" anything but simple.

Dr. Moberly is in his own way saying exactly what Bishop Gore said, "An authoritative mission is essential for all evangelistic work," and is supporting the view that "authoritative mission" is only to be found in episcopal commission.

If we accepted those expressions universally, as they are apparently used, all our experience of the ministry of which I have spoken would be contradicted; but it is certain that we cannot so accept them. I do not believe that either Bishop Gore or Dr. Moberly would have used them as they did, if they had been thinking of the facts of the mission field. In the cases of which we have been speaking, ecclesiastical commission was absolutely out of the question; and yet we cannot doubt that the ministry

---

14. Ibid., 163–64.

exercised by these men was a right ministry, and that they exercised it because they were moved by the Holy Ghost.

But if we are thus convinced that the speech of Bishop Gore and Dr. Moberly must not be carried outside of the limits within which they were speaking, we must not be hasty to conclude that we can carry over their expressions, and arguments concerning the celebration of the Lord's Supper, outside the limits within which they are speaking.

Of the men of whom we have been thinking, those who received their first instruction from members of the Anglican Church, or of some Church in communion with it, have learned that it is not the custom for unordained men in our native missions either to baptize or to celebrate the Holy Communion, and it is often desire for baptism which leads them to appeal to a foreign missionary; among white men of our own race it is held to be a custom that a layman may baptize in the absence of a priest but may not celebrate the Holy Communion, and it is generally desire for the Holy Communion which leads them to appeal to the bishop: but those who received their lessons from members of Christian bodies whose custom it is that any Christian may in case of need "Break the Bread," have not been so restrained from observing the Lord's Supper. In Miss Cable's book, *Through Jade Gate*, for instance, we read of an evangelist named Dr. Kao who in Kansu established many congregations of Christians and apparently not only baptized his converts but taught them all to observe the Lord's Supper.[15] Miss Cable was invited to visit them and to instruct selected members in the Bible, and she did that for some months, and she writes as though she had lived all the

---

15. Though he provided no bibliographic entry, Allen apparently is referencing *Through Jade Gate and Central Asia: An Account of Journeys in Kansu, Turkestan and the Gobi Desert* by Mildred Cable and Francesca French. This work has had several publishers over the years. It is likely Allen was referring to the London publication of 1927.

time in a regularly organized Church, organized by the Chinese Christians themselves.

We must proceed then to enquire whether this was in any way improper, or whether it was exactly how Churches sprang up in early days which later received the regular episcopal ministry. We must enquire whether expressions used by these authorities on the ministry in England with reference to Holy Communion have any more application to our case than their expressions concerning the charismatic ministry of evangelists.

# CHAPTER 4
# THE PRACTICE OF THE EARLY CHURCH

I pointed out in my last chapter that there was amongst us today a charismatic ministry which irresistibly recalled to our minds the ministry of the prophets, evangelists, **pastors and teachers,** healers, of whom we read in the New Testament.[16] We found these charismatic ministers outside the limits of the regularly organized congregations, in the hills of Assam or in the interior of the Ivory Coast, or in the dominions overseas, in farms or townships or villages which the regular clergy had not been able to reach, always beyond the effective control of any ecclesiastical authority, and generally in their beginning unknown to any ecclesiastical authority. We saw too that among our own people individuals gathered their friends together for religious services. We saw that Anglicans under such conditions hesitated to celebrate the Holy Communion and we said that we must consider whether there was evidence that Christians in early days felt any such hesitation. We are discussing our own case, and it may help us if we [not only] find that there is no evidence that they did not celebrate the Lord's Supper, but that on the contrary, what evidence there is suggests that they certainly did.

We must not expect to find much direct evidence; because, if, **as I believe, that was the normal practice, and** Christian

---

16. One of the original documents includes "pastors and teachers," while the other one has the words marked out. Since the other editorial markings differ on the corresponding pages of both manuscripts, I am unable to determine whether the words were to be removed or the editor later decided to include them.

writers took it for granted that the Christian rites were accepted and observed by Christian people, where there were no ordained ministers, it would be very strange if they went out of their way to assert it or to call attention to it.[17] They do not call attention to the normal accepted facts, in the organized Churches, except by allusion, or as the basis of some lesson which they wish to draw. In the Epistles of St. Paul, for instance, we do not find definite assertions that Christians were baptized as if that was news to anyone; we find baptism taken for granted and referred to as the basis of some argument, as for instance, in the expression, "Are ye ignorant that all we who were baptized" (Romans 6:3) were . . . .?[18] Or in the recollection of the fact that "I did not baptize" many (1 Cor 1:14–16). And similarly with regard to the Lord's Supper, St. Paul does not write to tell the Philippians that the Christians in Rome observed the Lord's Supper as if that would be any news to them, but that his imprisonment had caused members of the praetorian guard to hear the Gospel, which was news to them. It would have been strange if Christian historians of those days had told us that Christians observed Christian rites; and it is very strange that today a Christian priest should be writing to Christian men to tell them that they may do so, and arguing with them seriously as if to persuade them that they may do so. We must not then expect much direct evidence that the obvious actually happened.

In the New Testament itself we read that Philip the Evangelist went to Samaria and that many were baptized, and that the Apostles in Jerusalem sent Peter and John to visit them, who prayed for them and laid their hands on them and they received the Holy Ghost. The Apostles then went away. It is not said that Peter and John ordained any of them to minister, and the laying on of hands in this passage is never so interpreted. Did then the Church in Samaria not observe the Lord's Supper? Later St. Peter

---

17. One of the original documents include the words listed here, while the other document has them marked out.

18. Quoted from ASV.

went to visit "the saints" at Lydda and Joppa. At whose preaching these "saints" had been converted we do not know. Nothing is said of ordination. Did they not observe the Lord's Supper? Later we read that "they which were scattered abroad upon the tribulation that arose about Stephen traveled as far as Phoenicia and Cyprus and Antioch speaking the word," (Acts 11: 19).[19] Were these disciples, scattering in haste before a persecution, all ordained and commissioned to be evangelists, and given authority to ordain ministers to celebrate the Holy Communion for any who might be converted by their word? Or did those whom they converted not observe the Lord's Supper? Only in one case are we told; we know that the Christians at Antioch did so, at least the word "ministered" used about their services in Acts 13:2 is a word which the learned interpret particularly in that sense, and no one, so far as I know, questions that the Christians in Antioch did observe the Lord's Supper. Had they then been ecclesiastically ordained? All that we are told is that the Church in Jerusalem heard that Greeks were joining the Church in Antioch and sent Barnabas to see. There is no hint that Barnabas ordained anyone. On the contrary, Bishop Gore and Dr. Moberly affirm that the leaders of the Church in Antioch later ordained him.

When St. Paul went as a missionary into Galatia, we know that he ordained presbyters, but he did not remain long, and we know that Churches were multiplied throughout that region. Had those Churches no ministers who could celebrate the Lord's Supper? Did they not observe it? Did they wait for Apostolic ordination?

Long before any Apostle went to Rome, there were groups of Christians there meeting apparently in private houses, but St. Paul wrote to them as to one body. Did they not observe the Lord's Supper? They certainly observed baptism (Romans 6:3). Did Aquila and Priscilla, when they returned to Rome from

---

19. We are unable to determine the Bible translation that Roland Allen is quoting; it appears to be something in between ASV and KJV.

Corinth, discover the Christian observance of the Lord's Supper, which was certainly practiced in Corinth, a rite unknown in Rome?

So far as the New Testament carries us, the evidence, though slight, seems all on one side, and the conclusions irresistible. Christians who were scattered about the world could not possibly have been all ordained and commissioned by the apostles and they did not wait for any Apostolic ordination to observe the rite which Christ ordained for them.

After the New Testament comes "The *Teaching of the Twelve Apostles*" commonly called the Didache, a book which Bishop Gore says "we may assume to belong at latest to the first century" and "to have been composed by a Jewish Christian" probably in "some district remote from the centre of apostolic influence."[20] Now if it represents what was happening in remote districts, it represents what men in the early days thought was right for Christians who were exactly in our case.

Did the Christians spoken of in the Didache then, have no Eucharist; did they not observe the Lord's Supper, when they were beyond the reach of the regular ecclesiastical order of their day? Did the evangelists who first brought the faith of Christ to them teach them not to observe the Lord's Supper because they were not ordained by others who had themselves received ordination and commission from the Apostles of Christ?

That is not what we find in the Didache. There we find evangelists called Apostles, Prophets, and Teachers, who wander about, and Churches established by them whose local officers are called bishops and deacons and are elected. The Christians are instructed to meet and to observe a Eucharist; and if a Prophet visits them, they are to test him to find out whether he is a true prophet, but when they have decided that he is such, he is allowed to give thanks in the Eucharistic celebration without restriction. The Didache then bears witness to the truth of the deduction which

---

20. Gore, *The Ministry of the Christian Church*, 276–77.

we drew from the story of the Acts. The early Christians did not fail to observe the rite because they had not been ecclesiastically ordained, in the sense in which ecclesiastical ordination and commission is demanded today. We may agree with Bishop Gore that the Didache witnesses to extremely primitive and elementary conceptions of Christian doctrine and Christian Church order, but that does not lessen its witness to the universality of the practice of celebrating the Lord's Supper or to the independence of that practice of, say, restriction based upon a belief that the absence of regularly ordained ministers could deprive Christians of it.

It is true that Bishop Gore, taking it for granted that the laying on of hands, "gave, or confirmed the mission even of St. Paul and St. Barnabas," says that that example "will not allow us to suppose that the inspiration of these later prophets would have enabled them to dispense with ecclesiastical ordination by apostles or apostolic men,"[21] but there is no evidence whatsoever that they were actually commissioned or ordained by anyone, as he himself admits. They irresistibly recall to our minds those "evangelists" of whom I spoke in my last chapter. They were in the position of those men and they were as remote from "ecclesiastical ordination."

And here I want to call your attention to a fact which is very familiar to us. We know that that charismatic ministry of which I spoke in my last chapter is performed by men who possess a spiritual gift which was not conveyed to them by ordination. We see men sent out by authority to do the work of evangelists, but they cannot perform that work as the charismatic minister performs it unless they possess that charismatic gift. The difference is seen here: it is possible to direct the ordained commissioned evangelist to do the work of an evangelist; it would be absurd to direct a charismatic evangelist to do it. Who would have dreamed of telling Henry Kartyn to do the work of an evangelist—or Sundar Singh, or Harris, or Dr. Kao, or any other of the

---

21. Ibid., 285.

charismatic evangelists whom we know? The exhortation would seem ridiculous. But a man who has been commissioned and ordained for an ecclesiastical office can be exhorted to perform it. St. Paul could exhort Timothy to do the work of an evangelist. St. Paul could not make Timothy a Philip; he could ordain him to set in order Churches already established, and then tell him what to do. Within the circle of the Church a man can be ordained to an office; because in performing his office with the circle of the settled Church, he performs it. He performs it well or ill, but he performs it; when, for example, he celebrates, he celebrates, but outside that circle his ordination cannot supply the place of the charismatic gift. For that reason the charismatic gift recurs when Christian men are outside the circle of the organized Church, and recurs independently of any commission by ecclesiastical authority. It recurs independently, because the work must be done outside, beyond the reach of ecclesiastical authority, and because ecclesiastical authority, as I said before, cannot recognize those who possess the gift before they have revealed it in activity, so that it is impossible for ecclesiastical authority to ordain and commission beforehand all those whom God calls to do the work. The Apostles and Prophets of the Didache could not have been commissioned and ordained for their work, because before they did it, they could not be recognized, and after they did it, they were beyond the reach of ecclesiastical authority.

Thus far we have seen that in the early ages evangelists celebrated for their converts and taught them to elect officers to celebrate in their absence. But it may be said that the case of many of us is not covered by that. We are not charismatic evangelists, nor do we live in a group of Christians large enough and sufficiently settled to appoint officers for itself by election. Is there then any evidence which really corresponds to our case, the case of men who were communicants at home, and are now far away, and miss the Holy Communion? Is there any evidence that Christians like us ever celebrated the Holy Communion for themselves?

There is. But unfortunately Bishop Gore has so disputed it, that if I am to cite it, I am compelled to answer his arguments about it, and to show that the evidence is good evidence in spite of what he says. I am unwilling to do that, but I must do it.

The evidence is this. Tertullian, early in the third century, writing against the lawfulness of second marriages, which were then forbidden to priests, argues that laymen are bound by that law. "Where there is no bench of clergy," he says,

> you offer and baptize and are priest alone for yourself. Nay where three are, there is a Church, although they be laics . . . . Therefore, if you have the rights of a priest in your person when it is necessary, it behoves you to have likewise the discipline of a priest when it is necessary to use his right.[22]

Now that seems perfectly plain. Tertullian says that in his day men in our position did exactly what I am saying that we set out to do today.

Bishop Gore begins by saying that "Tertullian is here confessedly speaking about abnormal cases."[23] But why should those cases have been abnormal, any more than our destitution is abnormal today? Such cases can only have ceased to be common when there were few places in the Empire without a bench of clergy; otherwise almost every time that a Christian moved any distance from home he must have found himself in that case. So long as the Church was in the position of a missionary Church surrounded on all sides by heathen territory the case must have been common. Tertullian speaks of it as something quite familiar to his readers. Naturally; for if that was the custom of Christians in his day, it must have been a common custom. It must have been at least as common as our case. But Bishop Gore is not thinking

---

22. Ibid., 205.
23. Ibid.

of us and so he thinks of a position as abnormal which we know to be an everyday common experience.

Bishop Gore not only thinks of the case as abnormal, but he argues that what Tertullian asserts was really unknown to orthodox Christians. He uses three arguments to prove that:

(1) "Tertullian," he says, "is writing as a Montanist; that is, as one of a body which was setting itself against the Church, as in other respects, so also in reference to the authority of episcopal ministry,"[24] and after sketching some characteristics of Western Montanism, he concludes, "as well, then, might one quote the contemporary humanitarians as illustrating what had hitherto been the Church's doctrine about Christ, as the Montanists to illustrate here a doctrine of orders."[25]

That argument is liable to the answer that in this place Tertullian is not making any claim for the layman as against the Episcopal ministry. He is simply making a statement which he plainly expects his reader to admit. If a humanitarian writing against Catholic Christians made the assertion, you accept St. John's Gospel as an inspired record, therefore you must admit that Christ felt human weariness, because St. John says that He sat at Jacob's well because He was weary with His journey; that would be quite good evidence that the Christians to whom he was writing did accept St. John's Gospel. The fact that the writer was a humanitarian and held many unorthodox views would not affect the evidence from his words. If Tertullian was writing, as admittedly he was writing, to Catholic Christians, the fact that he was a Montanist does not affect in the least the force of his evidence when he says "you offer, you baptize."

(2) In a footnote he uses another argument. He says,

> Tertullian speaks of course as if his opponent would grant his position. But Tertullian though

---

24. Gore, *The Church and the Ministry*, 187–88.
25. Gore, *The Ministry of the Christian Church*, 213.

he is a very powerful is not a fair arguer, and it cannot be the least concluded that, when Tertullian uses or implies a "Nonne," his opponent would have answered "Yes."[26]

That seems to me a very strange argument with which to rebut Tertullian's assertion of fact in this case. "Tertullian," says Bishop Gore, "is a very powerful arguer." It is surely not the way of "powerful arguers" to base their arguments upon statements as of fact to men who know perfectly well that the supposed fact is not fact. Tertullian says, "you offer, you baptize: therefore you are bound by a law of the priesthood."[27] If the obvious answer was, "I do nothing of the sort," Tertullian's whole argument would have fallen to the ground. But do "powerful arguers" put up a case which can be overthrown as completely and as easily as that; and do they put it in a form which invites that crushing answer? Powerful arguers do indeed often state as facts what they themselves know to be no facts, but not when they know that their hearers, or readers, know the facts, nor in a form which compels them to recall the facts. If Bishop Gore was going to maintain that Tertullian's assertion was untrue he ought not to have called him a "powerful arguer," by way of convincing us that he was a weak one.

(3) Finally, Bishop Gore adds a third and totally different argument.

It needs to be remembered that, on all showing, a private Christian of Tertullian's day could *receive the sacrament* at home. Thus he could 'play the priest for himself', at least by giving himself the sacrament. It is not impossible that Tertullian has nothing more than this behind his argument.[28]

---

26. Ibid., 206, note 2.
27. If this is a direct quote, we have been unable to locate it.
28. Though Allen failed to provide the source of this quote, it may be located in a footnote on page 187 of Gore, *The Church and the Ministry*.

If we admitted that as an explanation of Tertullian's words what would remain of Tertullian's argument? The whole point of the argument is that the layman performs certain priestly acts, when he is out of reach of the clergy—acts which the priest performs, not acts like intercession, for instance, which any layman performs at any time when the clergy are at hand. What is the point of saying you do that where there are no clergy, if the act in question is one which laymen habitually performed where there were clergy. And what is the force of the following sentence, "Where three are, there is a Church, although they be laics"? And why argue at great length that Tertullian was a heretic when he wrote a sentence which any Catholic might have written, if it means what Bishop Gore suggests here? The defense that the words are the words of a heretic, if it had any force at all, and the defense that the words express a common Catholic practice are mutually destructive.

The evidence of Tertullian then remains, as I think, unshaken; but the character of the attack upon it shows us at once how remote from us is the thought of Bishop Gore and those who follow him. Would it have occurred to you that Tertullian's saying had anything to do with the rights, or the position, of the clergy? I suppose that you and I would simply have said that when men went where there were no clergy in those days the Christians did the best they could, just as in times and places when the Apostles were far away, the Christians were not necessarily without any sacraments, or ministry. The thing is entirely obvious and natural. Where the clergy are, there the ministrations of clergy are possible; where they are not, there the non-existent cannot exclude anything. The grace of Christ is wider than the episcopate. The promise of Christ that He will be with two or three gathered together in His Name is prior to the ordained ministry.

If evidence that the early Christians did not hesitate to use the sacraments of Christ in the absence of ordained clergy will help us, we certainly have sufficient evidence.

CHAPTER 5
# WE CANNOT GO BACK

In my last chapter I showed that if we desire support from the practice of the early Christians, the evidence is sufficient; but we are met with the objection that we are no longer living in the days of the early Christians and that consequently we cannot act now as they did then.

The obvious answer is that we are. In all the essential elements of the problem before us, we are back in their day. The mere fact that some centuries have passed does not make a difference in the spiritual needs of men, nor in the grace of Christ. We hear travelers say that when they get into the heart of Arabia they feel as if they were back in the days of Abraham or of Moses. What do they mean? They mean that the manner of life of the people whom they see there appears almost identical with the account given in the Old Testament of the manner of life of the people in the days of the Patriarchs. When I say that we are back in the first century I do not mean that we wear the same clothes or use the same speech, but that in the conditions of our life as Churchmen we find ourselves in the same position. As the early Christians were scattered, so are we; as the early Christians were remote from the ecclesiastical authorities of their day, so are we from the ecclesiastical authorities of our day; and as it is in this respect that we are back in the first ages of the Church, so we ought to use the Christian rites as those Christians used them under these conditions. The Christians of those days were not hindered by the remoteness of the ecclesiastical authority of the organized Churches of their day. We in like conditions, being in that sense back in their day, ought not to be hindered by the remoteness of ecclesiastical authority of our day. I have already pointed out that so far from being at hand at the moment when we need them, the ecclesiastical authorities are as remote from us as Bishop Gore says the ecclesiastical authority of the Apostles was from the Churches described in the *Didaché*. When we then act as they acted we do not go back; we simply recognize that we are back, and act accordingly.

Nevertheless I must examine the argument that we cannot go back; because when we are told that we cannot go back, many of us imagine that some insuperable barrier has been set up, in the centuries which have passed since those early days; and we imagine that what would really be a forward step for us would be a backward step, because it would be a backward step for an organized Church with a regularly constituted ministry.

I have already pointed out that Bishop Gore and Dr. Moberly are not thinking in terms of our position, but in terms of organized Churches with regularly constituted ministry. Their argument then would naturally seem to have nothing to do with us, but it is used none the less by many to intimidate us; and many of us are intimidated by it; for it is cited without any of Bishop Gore's or Dr. Moberly's reservations, but in its most rigid and absolute form; and some of us support a natural shyness of spiritual sloth by persuading ourselves that we have authority behind us, when we hear it in that form. It ought to be enough by itself to make us begin to question, if we find episcopal influence, and the arguments of theologians, on the side of irreligion fighting as the allies of spiritual sloth.

Dr. Moberly then is answering an objection which he expresses thus: "It may be said that even if individual inspiration be not the regular mode of appointment to ministry, yet it may validly stand side by side with a ministry of more regular method.

Does not the *Didache*, it may be asked, show clearly that it did so at the first? and if at the first why not now?"[29]

Here is it not plain that Dr. Moberly is thinking of a ministry which claims to supersede the regular ministry, or to stand "side by side" with it in the sense of side by side, at the same time, under the same conditions? Is he not thinking of a ministry which is making a claim against the regular ministry?

But that is not our case. We make no claim as against an ordained ministry. We do not stand "side by side" with it in that sense. We are not setting up a theory of ministry by inspiration against a theory of ministry by succession. We do not make any claim, nor set up any theory, nor argue that our ministry is based upon direct inspiration, and that therefore we can take the place of a regularly ordained ministry. We do none of those things, any more than a man in our position who tends a sick man is setting up a claim to be a doctor by divine inspiration, or even a nurse by divine inspiration. We are simply men, who being deprived of the assistance of the regular order, do the best that we can. We do not set up a theory of the superiority of the untrained, unqualified to the trained and qualified medical practitioner, because we help a man in distress to the best of our ability; neither do we set up a theory of the superiority of a charismatic ministry to the regularly ordained ministry because we do the best in our power in the absence of the regularly ordained ministry. Very few, if any, of those who have ministered to their fellows have even thought whether they are ministers by divine inspiration, or have attempted to justify their action by a theory of that kind. Such theories were not in their thoughts. They needed help, and they knew that they needed help, and they did what they could. An onlooker might well say that they were plainly moved by a spirit which urged them to seek help for themselves and to help others, but they themselves were

---

29. Moberly, *Ministerial Priesthood*, 108.

not thinking of that. They did not think that their action needed any justification and they did not stop to argue about it.

Proceeding with his argument Dr. Moberly says, "If it be granted, for the sake of argument, that the prophets of the *Didache* were unordained men, who superseded the ordained in the highest functions of their ministry," (That word "superseded" has no meaning in relation to us, nor I think in relation to the prophets of the *Didache*: unless it is possible to supersede the non-existent); "yet I should certainly not allow the principle to pass unchallenged, in abstract form, that what God did then He might at any time do";[30] and he cites the case of the sacrifice of Isaac as an example.[31]

We, of course, are not concerned to dispute that, "in abstract form." We are not dealing with abstractions but with practical matters of fact. We maintain that what God did at one time under certain circumstances and conditions, He has done again under like circumstances and conditions, and we are saying now, and all the time, that the conditions are present in which God did what He did, and therefore we are not surprised that He does it again.

"Direct interposition of the kind supposed," says Dr. Moberly, "might with perfect consistency be conceived as a consolidation of the infantine, and yet as a dissolution of the organized, Church."[32] But the Church did not cease to be "infantine" all over the world at the moment when in some parts of the world it ceased to be "infantine." The "infantine" stage exists side by side with the organized stage; and the Church was conscious of it so long as it was conscious that its members were pushing out into the heathen world, and "infantine" Churches were springing up. Only when it ceased to have that outward look and concentrated upon itself did

---

30. Moberly, *Ministerial Priesthood,* 109. Allen inserted the parenthetical statement inside this quote, providing his own commentary on Moberly's thoughts.
31. Ibid., 110.
32. Ibid., 109.

it forget the "infantine" and imagine that the organized was the whole. We now scattered about the world are in that "infantine" stage and know that it exists in our own persons, and what Dr. Moberly conceives as the "consolidation of the 'infantine'" applies exactly to us. He was not thinking of us, and therefore spoke as if the "organized" Church was the whole. Thus he left us—where? So far as his arguments went, we did not exist.

Elsewhere Dr. Moberly speaks of the miraculous gifts of the early evangelists as in some sort justifying their exercise of functions which later were confined to bishops and presbyters of the "organized" Churches; and in this place he says that if

> the personal claims of one of those men whom he thinks of as superseding the ministry of the regular clergy in the organized church, should seem to be vindicated by external corroborations, even to a miraculous sign made manifest in the heavens, it is at least an open question, on New Testament principles, whether the whole should not be treated far rather as an inscrutable delusion than as a veritable sign from God.[33]

It is true that our evangelists and pastors in our communities outside the "organized Churches" do not appeal to miracles to prove that they are doing God's work; **and that there is apparently this difference between this age and the age of the Apostles. But even in that age not all evangelists and prophets worked miracles.**[34] There is no evidence that a miracle was demanded as a

---

33. Ibid., 110. Though Allen quotes Moberly as stating, "The personal claims of one of those men whom he thinks of as superseding the ministry of the regular clergy in the organized church," these words are not found in Moberly's writing. Moberly's words, in this quotation, begin with "should seem" and continue to the end of the sentence with "God."

34. The typed manuscripts differ here. While both documents have proofreader's markings on these corresponding pages, one document

sign that a man was truly guided by the Spirit of God when he preached Christ and established Christian Churches with the rites of Christ. Christ our Lord Himself refused to do miracles as an external sign and proof of the approval of God for speech and actions which did not themselves in their own character bear the marks of divine grace. Of course a mere wonder would not prove that a man was doing the work of God. St. Paul, when a man questioned his apostleship, appealed to the character of his work, not to a mere miracle, saying, "You are the seal of my apostleship in the Lord." (1 Cor 9:2) This is the true test of any man's work; and this test is as valid today as ever. We need not then question whether we do or do not work miracles. A miracle would not justify us; the absence of miracles does not invalidate obedience to Christ.

But again it is urged that even if the early Christians did enjoy this liberty, the Church later restricted it, quite definitely and precisely. What was disallowed? The moment that we ask that question, we see once more that we and those who are supposed to be hindering our liberty are speaking of different things. Bishop Gore answers the question by saying, "the claim made by Tertullian"[35] in that passage which we discussed in the last chapter that laymen might in case of necessity offer.[36] But Tertullian in that passage made no such claim. He did not claim that laymen might offer: he simply asserted that they did. That word "claim" shows at once what Bishop Gore is thinking of. He is thinking of

---

removes and inserts some words here: "It is true that our evangelists and pastors in our communities outside the 'organized Churches' do not appeal to miracles to prove that they are doing God's work; but even in the Apostolic age not all evangelists and prophets worked miracles."

35. Gore, *The Church and the Ministry*, 112. Allen provides this reference, but I have been unable to locate this quote in Gore's book.

36. While Allen does not provide a direct quote here, margin notes include a reference to Charles Gore, "Reunion in South India," *The Church Quarterly Review* 110 (July 1930), 216. It is on this page that Gore wrote, "It is difficult to interpret exactly what Tertullian meant when he claimed for the layman in cases of necessity the right to 'offer.'"

a claim made by unordained or irregularly ordained men to perform an office as against the regularly ordained. And he says that that claim was disallowed. But if there was no such claim in the words of Tertullian, still less is there any such claim made by us. We make no claim against anybody.

"The claim is disallowed." When? and Where? The rule that only bishops and presbyters might celebrate the Eucharist was decreed wholly within the limits of the organized Church, and when any attempt on the part of the laity to do so would have been an open defiance of authority. All the examples and quotations upon which Bishop Gore and Dr. Moberly rely are wholly within that limit. Obviously. The rule became more rigid the more numerous and more powerful the regular clergy became, and the more the existence of any Christians wholly beyond the reach of the clergy became unusual, or forgotten. Whoever heard of a Church Council making decrees for Christians of whose existence it was ignorant? The decrees were made within the organized Church utterly regardless **of the possibility of** any Christians existing outside.[37] Did any Church Council ever deliberately pass any resolution with a view to disannulling the command of Christ or depriving Christians of the grace of the sacraments? The very idea of such a thing would have horrified the bishops who passed the decrees quoted today. Those decrees were passed to preserve the sacraments, not to annul them.

But then the custom grew up and the habit, and when the great modern expansion took place, the habit and the custom carried those decrees outside the limits for which they were designed and what was designed to be for life was turned to death.

There is another argument used by Bishop Gore and Dr. Moberly which is sometimes turned to our destruction, and terrified some of us. It is said that there is a Covenant. "Thus do. . .

---

37. One of the original typed manuscripts omits these words.

for thus God is pledged to receive you"[38] and that **only** acts of the regular clergy are within that Covenant.[39] I know that I must walk warily here, for Bishop Gore is careful to say men are dealt with according to their opportunities; and as God's love is not limited by His Covenant, so He *can* work through ministrations which have not the security of the Covenant, and Dr. Moberly is even more careful to avoid the danger of saying that the Covenant limits God's grace; but Bishop Gore goes on "But though God can do this, we have no right to claim it of Him,"[40] and that word "we have no right" terrifies some of us. We are told our action is outside of the Covenant and we have no right to claim God's grace outside of the Covenant, which is confined by the ministrations of the regular clergy. The Covenant is treated as a legal Covenant, circumscribed by a law, I am then compelled to protest against this use of the word "Covenant."

It is exactly parallel to the use of the word Covenant by the Judaizing party in the Church in St. Paul's day. They too maintained that there was a Covenant circumscribed by the Law within, in which all who would be secure of God's grace must stand. Against that St. Paul protested. He declared that the old Covenant which said, "Thus do, for thus God is pledged to receive you" was not the Gospel. The most important passage in which St. Paul uses the word is in Galatians 3, where he is contrasting the Gospel which rests upon a promise with the old Covenant which rested upon Law; and without question he uses the word Covenant in Galatians 3:15–17 of the Covenant of promise as opposed to the Covenant of Law, when he says "To Abraham were the promises spoken . . . Now this I say that the covenant confirmed before of God, the law which came four hundred and thirty years after doth not disannul." I do not think that the New Testament contains one reference to the covenant of promise

---

38. Moberly, *Ministerial Priesthood*, 64.
39. "Only" is written in one of the manuscripts.
40. Gore, *The Ministry of the Christian Church*, 110.

which suggests any such relationship to the Covenant of Law as it is suggested by "Thus do, for thus God is pledged to receive you." The promise is "Where two or three are gathered together in my name, there am I in the midst of them," Matthew 18:20, and "him that cometh to me I will in no wise cast out," John 6:37; and that promise a law which came in later cannot disannul so as to make the promise of none effect. The new Covenant of God is a promise; and acceptance of the promise and obedience to the command in expectation of the fulfillment of the promise is not without the Covenant, but within it.

Here again it is perfectly clear that neither Bishop Gore nor Dr. Moberly is using the idea of a Covenant, as they express it, against us, but nevertheless it is true that many interpret their language so as to exclude us, and to forbid us to obey the command or to claim the promise, telling us that what we do is without the Covenant; and so they terrify us. It is necessary therefore to insist that the Law which they invoke cannot disannul the promise; and that, when it is urged against us, it does not disannul the promise. That, neither Bishop Gore nor Dr. Moberly did.

It is plain then that when men say that we cannot go back to the practice of the early days, what they mean is that we cannot break a tradition, a custom, a habit, which has grown up within the regularly organized Churches and has then been held to bind men for whom it was never intended.

## CHAPTER 6
# THE PRIESTHOOD OF THE LAITY

We all agree that in the New Testament Christians are called to be a "royal priesthood" (1 Pet 2: 9) and "priests" (Rev 1:6; 5:10; 20:6); and that as a priestly race and priests they offer to God sacrifices of praise and thanksgiving; and that their observance of the Lord's Supper is so markedly an offering of praise and thanksgiving that it very early received the title of Eucharist.

We all agree that the ministers of the Church in that Eucharistic service act, not vicariously for the congregation, but representatively, and that it is the whole body which offers using an ordained minister as its mouthpiece. That word "mouthpiece" is not mine but Bishop Gore's.[41] "We bless the cup of blessing," "We break the bread" says St. Paul, speaking for the community; "we offer," "we present," is the language of the liturgies.

Most of us admit that it is quite impossible to prove from the words of the New Testament that there were any special officers to whom the function of acting as ministers in the Breaking of Bread and the Blessing of the Cup is definitely assigned, still less that there was any office which can be defined by that function; but most of us are equally certain that before very long that function was assigned definitely to bishops and priests, and that in the more highly organized Churches these officers were ordained only by bishops who had themselves been ordained in regular order. Where we seem to differ from those who exalt to the uttermost the tradition which is based upon that practice, and consequently

---

41. Gore, *The Church and Ministry*, 73.

speak of it as universal and immutable is in our refusal to apply it indiscriminately.

Bishop Gore and Dr. Moberly both make exclusive claims for the episcopal ministry in terms which, if they were thinking of us, would leave us absolutely hopeless and helpless. Bishop Gore, for instance, argues that a positive claim is, in a certain sense, necessarily exclusive; the position involves a negation. "'I am empowered by ordination to minister' implies that 'you who have no such ordination have no such power.'"[42]

Here if we forget, or fail to notice, that "in a certain sense," we shall read into Bishop Gore's words an absolute exclusion of all, everywhere, under any circumstances, who are not "empowered by ordination." But it is certain that when he was writing those words Bishop Gore was thinking of his "I" and his "you" as in one place and time: his "I" is speaking to his "you."

Dr. Moberly might seem to be making an exclusive claim for the episcopal ministry in the most absolute terms when, comparing the Church to the body and its ministers to the organs, he says,

> If any organs are missing, it does not follow that all the rest of the body put together can discharge the special functions which the missing organs were made to discharge. A body however otherwise complete cannot see without eyes, hear without ears, or run a race without legs. Still less does it follow, because the eye (say) is an organ of the whole body, living and seeing by, and not apart from, the body's life, that therefore any and every other member of the body severally has the same functional power as the eye for seeing.[43]

---

42. Ibid., 182.
43. Moberly, *Ministerial Priesthood*, 68–69.

That amounts to saying that if a Church by any means lost its episcopal ministry it would lose its sight absolutely. But we know in fact it does not, and we know that this analogy of the human physical body cannot be forced so to its logical conclusion. We must remember that Dr. Moberly himself has said in speaking of essential media that

> the necessity . . . is a necessity not simply self-acting, like the operations of a physical quality; it is a necessity, not of a material but of a moral kind; a necessity which, by its inherent character as moral, cannot but have real relations to varying conditions of understanding and of opportunity.[44]

The moment that we forget those qualifications and think of the episcopal ministry as "empowered" in an absolutely exclusive sense, so that we think that the functions which it performs cannot under any circumstances whatsoever be performed by anyone not so empowered, we really are concluding more than we have any right to conclude.

Dr. Moberly illustrates his position by the case of Naaman, and says,

> It would have been obviously futile for Naaman to have drawn a distinction, either, in respect of his own duty, between bathing in Jordan on the one side and obeying God on the other, or, in respect of his own blessing, between bathing in Jordan on the one side, and recovery from leprosy on the other. . . . It is the old distinction. If God is not in any way bound to His own appointed methods of grace, yet we are. Outside His appointed 'media' of whatever kind—ministries, sacraments, ordinances—He can work, if He will, as divinely as within them. He can cleanse with Abana, or with Pharpar, or with nothing, as

---

44. Ibid., 61–62.

effectually as with Jordan. But that is nothing to us,
if He has bidden us to wash in Jordan.⁴⁵

That argument plainly takes it for granted that the man who is told to wash in the Jordan can do so, if he will. But in our case Jordan has dried up. The episcopal ministry is not within our reach. We *cannot*, simply *cannot*, bathe in Jordan. The question then for us is whether we will bathe, praying that God will make that bathing efficacious for us, or whether we will not bathe at all. We are surely justified in thinking that God in telling us to bathe has not told *us* to bathe in *Jordan*.

Driven to its extremity the doctrine as set out by these theologians would make the sacraments entirely depend upon the will of a bishop, or upon his power of locomotion. A bishop could say to us, as in effect he does say today, "I cannot come to you, though you are in my diocese; I cannot, or I will not, ordain for you," and then the conclusion would follow inevitably that none of us are empowered to act, therefore Christ's sacraments are annulled for us. Is not that a *reductio ad absurdum* of the whole argument as applied to us?

Both Bishop Gore and Dr. Moberly speak of the priesthood of the laity; they both emphasize it; they both assert that the priesthood of the clergy is not to be separated from it; they both argue that an exclusive ministerial priesthood does not conflict with a corporate priesthood, or the individual priesthood, of all Christians. Bishop Gore, for example, expresses it like this:

The ministry is the instrument as well as the symbol of the Church's unity, and no man can share her fellowship except in acceptance of its offices. Why is this conception unreasonable? The people of Israel of old were a 'kingdom of priests, and an holy nation' (Exod. 19:6). But that priestliness which inhered in the race had its expression in the divinely ordained ministry of the Aaronic priesthood.⁴⁶

---

45. Ibid., 61.
46. Gore, *The Church and the Ministry*, 73.

He quotes Justin Martyr,

> Just . . . as Joshua, who is called by the prophet [Zech. 3:1] a priest, was seen wearing filthy garments . . . and was called a brand plucked out of the burning because he had received remission of sins, . . . so we, who through the name of Jesus have believed as one man in God, the Maker of all, have been stripped through the name of His First-begotten Son of the "filthy garments" of our sins; and being set on fire by the word of his calling are the genuine high-priestly race of God, as God beareth witness Himself, . . . saying that "in every place amongst the Gentiles men are offering sacrifices acceptable to Him and pure," and God receives from no man sacrifices, except through His priests.[47]

"Here," he says,

> is indeed a vivid consciousness of the priesthood which belongs to the Church as a whole, but which finds expression in a great ceremonial action—the Eucharist—an action which belongs not to the individual, but to the whole body, and is celebrated by the "president of the brethren";

and he asks:

> How, then, is this priesthood interfered with, if we should find reason to believe that Christ Himself ordained ministers of this mystical action . . . to be the mouthpieces of the Church in its celebration?[48]

---

47. Ibid., 74.
48. Ibid., 74-75.

Bishop Gore takes it for granted that the question can only receive one answer. But in our case the ordained priesthood, if it is used to exclude the operation of the other, does not only interfere with, but annul and destroy the priesthood of the laity. It is one thing to say that a priesthood functioning through a mouthpiece is not interfered with by the mouthpiece; it is quite another to say that the mouthpiece does not interfere with the priesthood of the whole body, if it is used to prevent it from functioning. To return to the analogy of the physical body which Dr. Moberly elaborated and Bishop Gore also uses:

> The ministry is the organ—the necessary organ— of these functions. It is the hand which offers and distributes; it is the voice which consecrates and pleads. And the whole body can no more dispense with its services than the natural body can grasp or speak without the instrumentality of hand and tongue."[49]

We all know that the whole body possesses a power of expression which is not confined to the instrumentality of hand or tongue; and it is the expression which is the important matter. Hand and tongue do not interfere with the expression, they assist it; but in their absence the body uses fingers in place of tongue, hooks attached to arms in place of hands. If absence of tongue was used as an argument to forbid the body to express itself, if absence of hand was used as an argument to forbid the body to touch and feel, then we should get the position which those try to force upon us who use the absence of ordained ministry to forbid the priesthood of the body to express itself. When they do that, the specialized ministry does war against the universal common priesthood of Christians.

\*\*As a matter of fact it is well known that the universal priesthood can perform the functions of the specialized ministry.

---

49. Ibid., 72–73.

Dr. Moberly looking back at the early ages, says that it did so [illegible word inserted by hand here]

It is not denied that the channels which existed from the first, and were more and more explicitly recognized as the channels divinely appointed for indispensable order, were at first too freely and too richly overflowed to be formally distinguishable as channels. . . . We do not therefore suggest that during the many consecutive years of St. Paul's imprisonment in Caesarea and in Rome there never was, because there never could have been, under whatever necessity, any fresh accession either to the ranks of the presbyters or to the number of 'confirmed' and communicant Christians. This is just the wrong sort of emphasis to lay upon what was doubtless establishing itself as principle before it was yet crystallized as rule. . . . We can hardly doubt that there was a period, while apostles were remote and the direct action of the Spirit was on all sides miraculously manifest, when consciousness as to limitations of outward method was not yet definite, and questions about the distinction of mediate or immediate exercise of apostolic government were neither asked nor answered. We do not deprecate a recognition of historical gradualness so obviously probable and lifelike as this.[50]

It is true that he continues, "What we do deprecate is the inference which is apt to be drawn, that the explicit consciousness of such outward principles and rules of method . . . was still—when it did become explicit as necessary rule—mistaken, or not necessary, or not expressly apostolic and divine."[51] But that can only be within the circle of the established Church.**[52]

---

50. Moberly, *Ministerial Priesthood*, xxv, xxvi, xxvii.

51. Ibid., xxvii.

52. This entire section is crossed out by the editor in one of the two originally typed manuscripts. Because there are other handwritten edits that differ between the two documents, it is unclear as to whether or not this passage was to be omitted from Allen's work.

Bishop Lightfoot, as is well known, maintained that the privileges of the specialized order could not annul the priesthood of the laity. "It may be," he wrote,

> a general rule, it may be under ordinary circumstances a practically universal law, that the highest acts of congregational worship shall be performed through the principal officers of the congregation. But an emergency may arise when the spirit and not the letter must decide. The Christian ideal will then interpose and interpret our duty. The higher ordinance of the universal priesthood will overrule all special limitations. The layman will assume functions which are otherwise restricted to the ordained minister.[53]

To this Dr. Moberly objects that

> This paragraph appears to combine two somewhat inconsistent lines of thought. The first runs thus. The layman is inherently a priest: and the universal priesthood is a 'higher ordinance' than the ministerial. It is therefore *essentially lawful* for the layman to perform all priestly functions; even though this essential and "higher" right may ordinarily submit, on lower grounds of convenience and expediency, to restriction. The second runs thus. Inasmuch as he has never received any commission which would warrant his doing so, it is *essentially unlawful* for the layman to minister. Nevertheless extreme emergencies may so

---

53. Allen's handwritten margin notes reference "Philippians p 266." The reader may find this quote in J. B. Lightfoot, *St. Paul's Epistle to the Philippians*, revised (Grand Rapids, MI: Zondervan Publishing House, 1953), 268.

over-ride all law as to make it spiritually right sometimes to do even what is, as long as law holds at all, positively and peremptorily forbidden.[54]

I am not concerned to defend Bishop Lightfoot's phraseology; but I must point out that it is Dr. Moberly who introduces the legal opposition (1) that it is essentially lawful for a layman to perform all priestly functions, (2) that it is essentially unlawful, but that in extreme emergencies he may do what is unlawful. The Christian, *qua* Christian, is a member of a priestly body and shares all the powers of the body, the universal being in the particular because the Spirit is one in the universal and particular. Therefore, when the Christian is with the organized body, he is with the organized body and must recognize the fact. He is not the whole body but a part, and can only exercise his priestly function as a part, with the other members and through the recognized mouthpiece of the whole. But when he is separated from the organized body, he, and any others who may be with him, are still priests because the Spirit is in them; and as Irenaeus said, "Where the Spirit of God is there is the Church and all grace";[55] and they must recognize that fact. Where they are, the universal still is. The moment that we treat episcopal ordination as one law and the universal priesthood as another, we fall to balancing the one against the other, as Dr. Moberly did, contrasting the law of ordination with the ordinance of the universal priesthood. But Bishop Lightfoot was not really doing that, though his language verbally

---

54. Moberly, *Ministerial Priesthood*, 90–91.
55. Allen does not provide a reference here. And while his quotation of Irenaeus is not exact, it is very close. The full quote is: "For where the Church is, there is the Spirit of God; and where the Spirit of God is, there is the Church, and every kind of grace; but the Spirit is truth" (Irenaeus, *Against Heresies*, book 3, chapter 24 in Alexander Roberts and James Donaldson, eds., *Ante-Nicene Fathers: The Apostolic Fathers, Justin Martyr, Irenaeus*, volume 1, American edition (Peabody, MA: Hendrickson Publishers, 1885), 458.

admitted to the charge. There are not two laws, but one, and that one, not a law like the law of the Sabbath, but a law like the law of love or the law of liberty, a gospel law, not a Mosaic law: and all that Bishop Lightfoot was saying was that one law reigns, whether through the ordained ministry, or through the unordained where the ordained does not, or cannot function.

We know well that Bishop Lightfoot's "emergency" is a very common emergency. It arises every day. We understand his "emergency" because it is our familiar condition. Dr. Moberly is not thinking in our terms and consequently he talks as if every Christian duty, which at home is assigned to the ordained clergy, were barred to us, and drags us all under the yoke of the law, which is really the Mosaic type. It is vain to set up an opposition between "essentially lawful" and "essentially unlawful" unless we keep all the time on the same plane, that is, within the Church as organized with ministers ordained by ecclesiastical authority. We are not on that plane. Where there is no ordained ministry, there can be no law confining religious functions to that ministry. That law can only obtain where there are those to whom it applies. Bishop Lightfoot's "emergency" recognizes that, and opens to us the door of grace.

Dr. Moberly accuses Bishop Lightfoot of what he calls the logical fallacy of concluding that because the whole Church is priestly, therefore each individual can act as a priest. "It would not be very good logic," he says,

> to confound the universal with the distributive "all." If "all Englishmen," i.e. universally, the total nation, could abolish rights of property, it does not follow that "all Englishmen," i.e. distributively, any one who is English, has the authority to abolish property.[56]

---

56. Moberly, *Ministerial Priesthood*, 72.

But "an emergency may arise," as Bishop Lightfoot says. Then what happens? Take not an uncommon emergency. It not infrequently happens that a number of sailors are separated from their ship either in boats, or on a raft, or on an island. Being men who cannot, and will not, at once fall into anarchy, having, that is, within them the common capacity of civilized men for law and order, they immediately, in the absence of the established government of the ship, proceed to provide themselves with a government and order. Either one of them by natural power of mind or body is accepted by the whole body, or the whole body appoints a leader, and that leader does abolish all rights of private property in provisions, if not in all other private possessions. He does it and does it rightly. He assumes all the power which under normal conditions he could not exercise.

Dr. Moberly's fallacy is a fallacy only so long as we remain on the same plane. He assumes in his argument that he is speaking of Englishmen under the normal conditions of Englishmen at home. The "emergency" puts everything on a different plane: the small group becomes for the moment a state, and its governor exercises the authority and power of a governor in a regularly organized state; and if the members of it are Englishmen, it is just because they are as Englishmen capable of ordered government that they do precisely what Dr. Moberly says they cannot do. The inherent power of government which is in them all emerges into practical activity. It is exactly so that in the absence of the regularly ordained priest the priesthood of the isolated group emerges, and the group organizes itself under its own priests, rather than to live in anarchy.

We see then once more that the arguments of those theologians who seem to exclude us have nothing to do with us, because they are not considering our case. Bishop Lightfoot at least considered our case as an emergency, though he evidently thought of it as something rare and exceptional; and the moment that he did so, he saw at once that what he called the higher, i.e. the wider and more inclusive, ordinance must overrule all special limitations which only apply within their own sphere.

If Dr. Moberly had been considering our case directly, instead of being engaged in rebutting what he saw only as a dangerous attack on the position of the episcopally ordained ministry, we have reason to think that he too would have taken the same line; for he writes,

> The necessity . . . which is asserted . . . is a necessity not simply self-acting, like the operations of a physical quality; it is a necessity, not of a material but of a moral kind; a necessity which, by its inherent character as moral, cannot but have real relations to varying conditions of understanding and opportunity; a necessity which appeals alike to our belief and our obedience, with a moral power indefinitely the greater, just because it is not either in all cases literally universal, or in any case visibly demonstrable.[57]

That sentence certainly suggests that the "necessity" of which he speaks is "necessity" only for those to whom he is speaking, that is, to those who can, if they will, have the services of an episcopally ordained ministry.

Episcopal ordination is not the one and only qualification for ministry; there are others, as Dr. Moberly has pointed out with notorious cogency. And to dwell on that one as if it were the only one of importance is not good for us, and may lead us into the very false action, even into denying the grace of our Lord to men who are beyond the reach of ordination or whose ordination may be hindered by a tradition not less legal and cruel than this.

---

57. Moberly, *Ministerial Priesthood*, 61–62.

## CHAPTER 7
# PRESUMPTION

I have now shown, and I hope that I have shown sufficiently, that in the early Church men did not wait for ordination by any ecclesiastical authority to empower them to observe the Lord's Supper when they were outside the range of the organized Church; that we today are in their position; and that the universal priesthood cannot be annulled by an absent specialized priesthood; but I know that there is widespread amongst us an idea that any exercise of that universal priesthood, except through the ordained ministry, is a presumptuous invasion of the functions of the ordained clergy, even where they admit that they cannot be. It is necessary, therefore, that we should face this bugbear, for bugbear is what it is, and settle with ourselves what this fear of presumption on our part really is, and how it arises.

Our conception of Christian ministry has been colored by the fact that we have looked at it solely as it took form in settled Churches. Looking at that alone we have set up a norm, and anything which does not conform to that norm we have either ignored or denied: we have either been blind to its existence, or we have denied that it is a ministry in any proper sense of that term.

That definition cannot be applied to the New Testament. If we consider the list of ministries given by St. Paul in Ephesians 4:11, apostles, prophets, evangelists, pastors, and teachers, or the list in 1 Corinthians 12:28, apostles, prophets, teachers, miracles, healings, helps, governments, divers kinds of tongues, we see at once what a large place is taken by gifts of ministries which suggest a ministry directed toward the conversion of those outside the Church. Apostles and evangelists are certainly ministers to the heathen; prophets and teachers and healers, probably for the most part; and tongues, as St. Paul himself tells us, are for a sign not to them that believe, but to the unbelieving.

We see also that these lists will not admit of tabulation either into localized and unlocalized offices, nor into any definite grades, nor into distinct and separate offices. The same persons might, and did, possess several of these gifts, or perform several of these functions, though many may have received only one of them, and have exercised only that one; the same persons exercised these gifts, or performed these functions, both within the settled Churches and outside them, though others may have exercised them only within the Church in which they lived; and that they are not arranged in any definite order is manifest, for we have only to compare the list of gifts in 1 Corinthians 12: 8–10, with the list given later in the same chapter, (verse 28), to see prophecy sixth in one list, and prophets second in the other, healings and miracles changing places, and many other variations, or we need only to compare the lists which I quoted above to see evangelists and pastors thrust in between prophets and teachers.

It is as impossible to make an orderly hierarchy of officers in the early Church from these lists, or to define the functions of each order by the gifts recited in these lists, as it is to catalogue the modern charismatic ministers of whom I spoke in the third chapter, and to define their functions by the titles given to them, or adopted by them.

If in looking at these lists we think of the ministry as it came to be defined in later years in settled Churches as the norm, and inquire by the light of that defined order what functions were allowed to this or that minister, possessed of this or that gift, in the early Church, we fall at once into the error of interpreting the fluid by the rigid. Christians exercised the gift, or the gifts, which they received, and nothing was "allowed" or "disallowed" as by any defined law governing their ministry, and prescribing the limits within which they could exercise it. Outside the Churches which had already definite officers with defined functions, they could perform any function, and even when they visited Churches with definite local officers they were welcomed and given the privilege of the highest officers, if their work proclaimed them to be true ministers of the Gospel. That is what we see in the case of Apollos in the New Testament as well as in the Didache.

Any theory of the ministry, then, which forgets that ministry of expansion, and attempts to compel the words of the New Testament to fit a hierarchy with defined functions, must necessarily find the task difficult, and its conclusions doubtful.

Nevertheless it is inevitable that this should occur. Churches which at first were isolated and self-organized, or organized by a wandering evangelist, naturally sought to follow the example of Churches which had been established before them, and had a longer history and more carefully defined organization, and country Churches naturally desired to imitate as far as they could the example of the town Churches. As the Churches of the expansion came into closer contact with the Churches of a more clearly defined character, their ministry was settled after the model of the more sharply defined ministry; and the ministry of expansion came to be remembered by them only as an early stage in the history of their ministry.

Thus the defined ministry becomes the only proper ministry, and any ministry which does not conform to the rule established is denied the very title of ministry, as if the ministry of expansion ought to have ceased to exist everywhere when Christian communities which were themselves the fruit of it left it behind them.

The formally organized ministry cannot admit any ministry which does not come within the terms of its definition. As I pointed out earlier, the language of writers within the limits of the organized Church, with its sharply defined ministry, seems inevitably to exclude it. I pointed out that the language used by writers like Bishop Gore and Dr. Moberly would seem to exclude it absolutely. You remember the words, "Any aspiration to ministry in Christ's Church, or attempt to discharge its duties, however otherwise well-intentioned, would be a daring presumption."[58] And "an authoritative mission is indeed essential for all evangelistic work, for 'how shall men preach except they be sent?'—how, that is, can anyone take upon himself so responsible an office?" and you remember how these writers stressed the laying on of hands at Antioch as "giving or confirming the mission" even of St. Paul, in order to impress the lesson on us.[59]

But the ministry of expansion, the charismatic ministry, is not so to be suppressed. It breaks out again and again. As we saw in an earlier chapter, it appears unbidden and undirected. It is impossible to say that it ought not to exist, that the only missionary ministry which ought to exist is a ministry sent out formally by ecclesiastical authority with well defined functions and rights, each in its several order. So long as the Church is expanding, the ministry of expansion must recur, as it does recur, because so long as the Church is expanding, the expansion must outrun the ecclesiastical authorities.

I speak, then, to those who have acted without any ecclesiastical ordination. Did it ever occur to you for one moment that you were guilty of any presumption? Can you imagine for one moment that the others of whom I spoke were guilty of any presumption? It is certain that with one voice both they and you would say that presumption was utterly remote from your thoughts. But was there any presumption, though you did not think of it? Ought you to have waited until you could receive a commission from some ecclesiastical authority before acting as you did? You will answer, "If I had, I should not have acted at all." "But," it may be said, "others have waited." To that you reply, "I could not wait. For me

---

58. Moberly, *Ministerial Priesthood*, 102.

59. The first quote is from Gore, *The Church and the Ministry*, 211; the second we have been unable to locate.

it was a question of acting at once, or failing to do what I felt to be my duty."

By what authority did you dare to gather your neighbors for prayer, or preach Christ to the heathen? If anyone had asked such a question you would have said, "I did not know that I needed any authority to do that. I just felt that I must do it." And if the questioner had pressed his point and demanded "Do you mean to say that you today claim to be a charismatic minister?" you would probably have answered, "I do not know what you mean by a charismatic minister: I just did what I felt I ought to do." And if he had said "A charismatic minister is one who acts as a minister solely as moved by the Holy Ghost," I think that you would have answered, "Well, if you choose to put it like that, I suppose that it was the Holy Spirit who urged me to do what I did, for I do not think it can have been any other spirit."

But good theologians, like Dr. Moberly and Bishop Gore have stated in the most universal terms that any such ministry is impossible and inconceivable today, and that not even the working of miracles would prove that you had any such authority as you claim. You would have replied, "I cannot help that, and I do not believe it. I think that if Dr. Moberly or Bishop Gore had been here he would have said that I did quite right."

And Dr. Moberly and Bishop Gore would have said so. They were not thinking of you when they wrote as they did. Yet many men in your position have felt that it would be an act of presumption to dare to hold a service of any kind, and have said that they were not going to set themselves up as "parsons."

You saw through that, and you knew that it would be well if all Christian men in your position acted as you did. You saw that that fear of presumption was a bugbear and it did not terrify you because you were impelled by a spirit which drove it off the field. You knew that you were not setting yourself up to be a parson, though you could not have denied that you were in fact performing a function, whether holding a service, or in preaching, or in guiding and advising the members of your congregation, which is, in a settled organized Church, commonly held to be a function of the ordained minister. You were not an ordained minister, but you knew that you were empowered to act by the spirit which moved you to act.

Exactly the same argument applies to the administration of the Lord's Supper. You know that you need the Sacrament; you know that it would help all those who join with you, and that its observance would bind you all together in the service of Christ. Can you then allow yourself to be hindered by a fear of presumption?

You know that there are fearful souls who cannot, or will not, find rest, because they say, or think, that they are not fit to receive the grace offered to them by Christ. And you know the answer: Christ's grace is promised to sinful men; He came to save sinners; and He promised, "he that comes to Me I will in no way cast out" (John 6:37). That is the answer which you give; and if anyone says "Oh I could not presume upon that," you point out that it is no presumption to take Christ at His word, and to believe His promises, but that, on the contrary, it is great presumption to disbelieve Him. So it is here. You believe that Christ told you to observe His Last Supper; you believe that He said, "Where two or three are gathered together in my name there am I in the midst of them." Is it not then greater presumption to disobey Him than to obey Him?

But you say, "I have been taught all my life that no one but an ordained priest can consecrate the elements." What did they who taught mean by "consecrate the elements"? In what sense did they say that an ordained priest could consecrate the elements? Have you not learned that it is God alone who can "consecrate" in the sense of making the elements become to those who receive them the means whereby we partake of His Body and Blood? Have you not observed that that prayer, which is called in our prayer book the prayer of consecration, is a *prayer*, and that it is spoken in the name of the whole congregation? How then can the priest be said to consecrate? That can only be said in a subordinate sense. It is not his personal act; neither does he perform his part as an individual. Is there then any reason to believe that prayer offered by the little group of which you are a member would not be heard and answered, because none of you have been ordained? And may you not offer a sacrifice of thanksgiving? Do you really believe that Christ would not hear you nor receive you because you have no episcopally ordained priest among you? We settled that question in the first chapter.

The idea that a priest is "an individual with special power" apart from the body of the Church of which he is a representative and mouthpiece is a late conception. In earlier ages dioceses were small, and the bishop was the representative of a Christian community which knew him, and which he knew personally. "The priesthood," says Bishop Gore, was

> kept more closely in connection with the Church or community. . . . Later—owing to the more independent position which the circumstances of large dioceses gave to the presbyter—his substantive priesthood, inhering in him as an individual, comes to the front. A presbyter is not so much a man who occupies a certain position and grade in the hierarchy of the community; he is an individual with special powers. His priesthood had become detached.[60]

Bishop Gore, with his eye fixed on the succession, finds here a "change of ideas, but it is not in any way fundamental."[61] In relation to the succession it is not fundamental, but in relation to the position of the clergy it is fundamental. To it we must ascribe

---

60. Gore, *The Ministry of the Christian Church*, 180–81.

61. Ibid., 178. Between this sentence and the next, one of the two typed documents includes the following typed statement: "I should have thought that such a change was peculiarly fundamental."

our modern habit of thinking of the celebration of Holy Communion as the act of an individual charged with special powers, the congregation being passive recipients, rather than as the act of a Church which meets to perform its own proper rite. An individual possessed of these special powers is sent to celebrate for a Church to which he may be a complete stranger, or known only as an occasional visitor. He celebrates, not as the representative and mouthpiece of the Church there present but as exercising powers conferred upon him as an individual. The result is a great gulf between the priest and the Church, which loses the realization of its true corporate existence, and an expression like "only a priest can consecrate the elements" takes the place of "we offer," "we present," in the thought both of clergy and laity.

To it we must ascribe the practice of sending "an individual charged with special powers" to travel round a great area ministering to Christian groups; with the result that in the intervals between his visits the Church ceases to exist in each of the groups. In his absence the Christian folk are as destitute as if no priest existed.

To it we must ascribe the practice of modern bishops who, ruling over vast dioceses, leave large numbers of groups without any ordained priests. In earlier days, "whenever any number of converts were made, as soon as they were capable of being formed into an organical Church, a bishop, or a presbyter, with a deacon, was ordained to minister to them."[62] That was because ecclesiastical authority then looked at the group as a body to be organized at the earliest possible moment. If that were so with groups of new converts how much more would it have been so with groups of Christians who migrated and settled in a new district?

But today the ecclesiastical authority looks not at the group but at individuals, and, looking at individuals, makes demands which no member of the group can satisfy. Since none of them can

---

62. Here Allen provides the following citation in the margin: "Bingham, Bk I Cap V Sec. 4." This is a quote from Joseph Bingham, *The Antiquities of the Christian Church*, Book 1, (London: Henry G. Bohn, 1856), 13.

satisfy the demands none of them can be ordained, and the whole group is left destitute, instead of being established as a Church.

That is the reason why I am compelled to address this little book to many who are not wholly beyond the reach of a bishop even in those vast areas which we today call dioceses. They are deprived of all that Church life which ordained priesthood suggests, almost as much as those groups which really do lie wholly beyond the reach of any bishop. This book ought properly to be addressed only to Christians who are geographically beyond the reach of any bishop; but the modern practice is so universal that what I say to them applies to others who ought never to be in their case.

The idea that priesthood consists in special powers conferred upon individuals by authority lies at the back of their fear of presumption, which so many of us feel. We feel it, because there is truth in it. There is truth in it within the order of regularly organized Churches. There individuals are ordained, and special powers are not conferred upon them as individuals apart from the Church, but as individuals within the Church; and that they do not possess them as a private possession, but as the representatives of the Church, to be used within the Church; but they do possess them. From that it is supposed to follow that those who have not received that gift and that authority cannot exercise that function under any circumstance without presumption. If they have not received the gift and the authority, they have not, and there is an end.

But I have already shown that that is not true if it is pressed outside its proper limits, that is, outside the boundary of the organized Church within which that priesthood is not refused, but established, within which that priesthood does not annul the commands of Christ, but maintains them. The moment we pass that line, and the necessity of that priesthood is carried so far as to annul the commands of Christ to all who do not, because they cannot, have it, that moment it ceases to be true, and men unordained, who then follow the commands of Christ, are guilty of no presumption. There is all the difference in the world between assuming the functions of an ordained priesthood when present, and recognizing its non-existence where it is non-existent, and in acting accordingly. The one is presumption, the other is not.

The ideas that the non-existent can exclude men for the Sacrament, and that no charismatic ministry can exist today, or that, if it does, it cannot celebrate the Lord's Supper, are generally supposed to be connected with the doctrine of Apostolic Succession. They are deeper than that, and wider. They hold men who utterly reject the doctrine of Apostolic Succession. You can see that for yourselves. The Congregationalists certainly do not hold that theory; and most of the Presbyterians do not; the Methodists do not; yet in the mission field they certainly do not admit the right and authority of any Christian, or of any congregation, to celebrate the Lord's Supper nor even to baptize. They certainly do not teach their converts to practice those rites for themselves. And though many of them do in theory admit the right of every Christian to break the Bread, yet as their ministerial body grows numerous and powerful, so the rites are more and more restricted to the ordained ministers, so that even among their own scattered members you find many groups which do, as a matter of fact, wait for the administration of those rites until one of their ordained ministers appears on the scene, just exactly as our own people do. If I had been a member of one of those bodies, I might have written what I have written with only the change of a few expressions. An ordained stipendiary ministry always tends to restrict the performance of certain functions to its own order, whatever theory of the ministry might hold. The idea that there is some presumption on the part of anyone else who performs these functions grows as the ordained ministry grows in numbers and self-consciousness. The theory follows, and, whatever form the theory takes, it takes the form of fostering this idea of presumption.

In our own communion that notion of presumption is often supported by an argument drawn from the text, "No man takes this honor unto himself," (Heb 5:4), with the addition that "the only evidence within our cognizance of the fulfillment of this condition is the fact that the minister is called according to a divinely-appointed order," and by "a divinely-appointed order" is meant ordination by recognized authority.[63]

Now in our experience that is not true. So far from being the only evidence, it is not by itself sufficient evidence. What we find is something very different. The evangelist speaks, or the farmer calls his family and his neighbors to prayer, and no one asks about appointed order. They say, "This man speaks the words of God," and "This man is a good man, and helps us."

The evidence on which we rely is not order in the sense of ordination according to an appointed order, but a manifestation of the Spirit. When we meet it we are satisfied that the man did not take any honor to himself, and we say "This man was called of God." On the other hand we sometimes meet with men ordained according to the appointed order who convince us that they did take this honor to themselves (a bishop being, so to speak, the instrument which they used to attain it), and then, in spite of the evidence of ordination, we say, "This man took this honor to himself." Thus when we are told to accept the evidence of ordination as the only evidence within our cognizance, the facts of our spiritual experience refute it.

"Called according to a divinely-appointed order" is only evidence in strict relationship to the order, under the rule. "The powers that be are ordained of God."[64] The evidence of ordination is sufficient within that order, and indeed within that order is the only evidence sufficient. But on the other hand the evidence of Divine call without that order is sufficient for those without that order, and is indeed the only evidence which is sufficient for them. The evidence is sufficient for them, but not within the order. In

---

63. We are unable to locate a source for these quotes.

64. Roland Allen did not provide a source for this quote, but it can be found on page 349 of Gore's *The Ministry of the Christian Church* and on page 308 of Gore's *The Church and the Ministry*.

the order, that evidence is wholly inadequate, and no amount of evidence of that kind can within the order suffice, as Bishop Gore and Moberly contend. If a man is not called within the order by due appointment no other evidence is admissible.

Thus it is vain for those who write of the order within the order to make an exclusive claim for that order outside it, because the spiritual experience of men outside it refutes the claim. They meet and know a ministry which they recognize as a ministry divinely appointed, in spite of the fact that it is not ordained within the order. But it is equally vain to answer the exclusive claims made for the ordained by appeal to that experience, for that experience is outside the order, and has no meaning as evidence for the man who speaks from within. When one without disputes with one within, and each speaks his own language, they do not understand one another.

But that was not always so. In the New Testament and in the Apostolic age, as we have seen, no sharp line of division was drawn between the two, no conflict was emphasized, no war waged. We today are back to that point, and in our case the same harmony ought to reign; for our ministry is in no way opposed to the ministry ordained in succession, but should rather prepare the way for it, as it did in those early ages. Our experience ought to teach us once more to understand the New Testament, and to understand the relationship which should exist between the ministry of expansion and the settled ministry, and to express each in terms which do not conflict.

There is then no "presumption" in our case. There is no setting up of ourselves against the ordained ministry, no assumption of powers which do not belong to us, no self-assertion either against man or God. That God is not unwilling to receive our sacrifice of praise and thanksgiving, and to grant us His grace, we know; that Christ will accept and bless us, we know. That a priest, or even a bishop may not upbraid us we are not so certain, but at least we are certain that we are not trespassing upon their reserves, any more than those derelict sailors of whom we spoke in the last chapter were trespassing upon the rights of the justices of England, or the prerogatives of the Houses of Parliament when they accepted, or set up, a leader who should settle their disputes and divide out their property for the common good to the best of his ability.

If anyone argues that we are deserting our Bishop, or transgressing his government, when we act for ourselves, our answer is plain. Let him appear and let him exercise his office and we will receive him and do him reverence.[65] We only wish he would do so. We do not desert him any more than those derelict sailors deserted their captain. When we act for ourselves we are only meeting the plain facts of our life, of which the one relevant fact in this matter is that the bishop is not here. If, and when, he appears, then we shall be in a different position, and shall face the changed conditions as we ought to do; but now they are not here, and we cannot deal with the non-existent. There is no presumption in facing plain facts and acting accordingly.

If Robinson Crusoe on his island sang, "I am monarch of all I survey," he was guilty of no presumption, because though there were many monarchs in the world, and one to whom he owed allegiance in his own country, he could yet say, "my right there is none to dispute." Presumption must be related to some person, either a man whose position the presumption infringes, or God, whose truth the presumption transgresses; and with us, as with Crusoe, there is none such. Then there is no more presumption in our case than in his.[66]

---

65. In one of the typed manuscripts, the unedited text reads: "Let him appear and let him according to his office ordain, and we will receive him and do him reverence."

66. In one of the typed manuscripts, a portion of this paragraph is omitted with editorial marks on other phrases. The statement regarding Crusoe is crossed out and the paragraph reads: "Presumption must be related to some person, either a man whose position the presumption infringes, or God, whose truth the presumption transgresses; and in our case, there is none such."

The one test of presumption is this: Where episcopal ordination maintains the command of Christ, and assists His people to obey Him and to receive His grace, there it is presumption on the part of any other to assume the function of the ordained minister; but where a supposed necessity of ordination hinders Christians from obeying Christ, and receiving the grace of the Sacraments, there is a delusion and a snare, and in setting it aside is no presumption.

"Let us therefore come boldly to the throne of grace, that we may obtain mercy, and find grace to help in time of need" (Hebrews 4:16).[67] We lay folk ought to feel no more fear of presumption in celebrating the Holy Communion than in reading morning or evening prayers, or in administering baptism."***

---

67. Quoted from WEB.

*** At the recommendation of Hubert Allen, grandson of Roland Allen, we have changed the order of the last two paragraphs of the original text, in order to make for a more complete sounding end of the manuscript.

# POSTSCRIPT

*The Ministry of Expansion* was written in the late 1930s and was not Allen's last writing on the subject of our discussion. In 1943, he wrote what became known as *The Family Rite*, which was never published during his lifetime. This latter work revealed the development of his thoughts regarding who could administer Communion. David M. Paton published the document in *Reform of the Ministry* in 1968. Paton's book, at the time of this writing, remains in print with The Lutterworth Press and should be consulted by the reader. However, before concluding *The Ministry of Expansion* and reading *The Family Rite*, Robert Banks' postscript serves as an excellent transition between the two. This introduction is a bridge between the late 1930s and early 1940s in Allen's ecclesiology and missiology.

## *THE FAMILY RITE:* AN INTRODUCTION

Robert Banks

I first came across the three volume collection of Roland Allen's writings, *Missionary Method's: St Paul's or Ours*, *The Spontaneous Expansion of the Church*, and *The Ministry of the Spirit*, issued by the World Dominion Press, over four decades ago. Just two years out of theological college, I was serving as an assistant in a large city Anglican church. During this time, I was beginning to experience some genuine difficulties, at both a theological and practical level, about the ordained ministry, church structures, and Christian mission. Although these difficulties were basically generated by a constant reading and re-reading of Paul, they were confirmed or extended by the writings of such people as the biblical scholar Eduard Schweizer, the theologian Emil Brunner, and the missiologist Roland Allen. Some two years later, my changing convictions—about the role of the laity in ministry, church as face-to-face edification, service and community, the vocation and mission of all believers in the world—led to my resignation from the Anglican ministry. Out of this I gradually became involved in a more organic, grassroots approach to church life and in resourcing lay life and mission through believers' everyday work, situations, and relationships, as well as through their voluntary, cultural, and civic activities.

It was only a few years ago, however, in David Paton's collection of Allen's largely unpublished essays, under the title *Reform of the Ministry*, I first came across his embryonic thoughts on Communion or what is called there, echoing his words, "The Family Rite." Though these thoughts were penned in 1943,[68] he clearly had been wrestling with them both practically as well as theologically from the time of his resignation from officially functioning in Anglican parishes several years before. *The Family Rite* also briefly discussed paid ministry, denominationalism, and religious tolerance, but I was interested chiefly because over the previous thirty years, I had regularly experienced Communion in more informal, familial-like ways and settings as a result of my longstanding house church involvement. It was encouraging to discover Allen's willingness to challenge church practice and missionary methods in this area.

In doing this, Allen demonstrates again how perceptive and prescient he was. He argued that, because it was essentially a family affair, the most appropriate setting for the Lord's Supper or

---

68. The first margin note in Allen's unpublished, handwritten manuscript of *The Family Rite* reads, "I was born in 1868 and it is now 1943."

Communion was not the church building but the home. This was the case in the earliest Christian communities, and it was by degrees over a long period of time that it changed its character and became more of a temple-like event in an ecclesiastical setting.

Allen believed it was time to return to the original practice, especially in situations where there was no public organized service available. Even where available, he argued for family rather than parish celebrations of Communion because they were less individual acts of devotion and more genuinely relational. Accordingly, the one who was to preside at this Sacrament was the head of the household rather than the ordained minister: it was a lay, rather than clerical, prerogative—something already recognized for baptism in certain circumstances—and as such, a ministry that should be returned to the ordinary people of God. Though, for practical reasons, for him celebrating Communion this way was mostly limited to himself, his wife, the occasional visitor, and wider family; ideally it was to involve others as well, and families should, from time to time, join one another to celebrate it. The most appropriate way of doing this was by dressing informally, drawing from the Prayer Book, but in a flexible way suitable to particular occasions, and connecting it to a meal, such as breakfast or dinner.

In advancing these views, Allen preceded the work of those biblical scholars and theologians from shortly after the middle of the last century who insisted that the Lord's Supper was originally based in believer's houses (cf. Acts 2), as they met together as the church in the home (cf. Acts 20, 1 Cor 11). Also that this was most likely hosted by the primary person or persons in the household, not necessarily the man alone but perhaps both husband and wife. Allen's practice also foreshadowed the holding of Communion in the more informal types of church life, such as house churches, basic ecclesial communities, and cell groups in many parts of the world from the sixties onwards—as well as in some cases by families themselves in domestic settings.

In two respects Allen also differed from the writings and practice of those who came after him. First, although he believed there was biblical precedent for his views on Communion, he was initially provoked to take the step mainly because of a moral objection to receiving Communion from the hands of salaried ministers of an ecclesiastical institution, though this too for him had a theological dimension. Later authors and believers were more compelled by biblical theological imperatives. Second, in discussing the New Testament, most of the writers and believers mentioned above argued that the Lord's Supper or Communion was an actual, not just ceremonial, meal. It involved ordinary food and drink, and sacramentally it was not just the elements but the whole meal, including the interchange between God's people during it, through which Christ was vitally remembered, actively present and more fully anticipated.

Had Allen lived long enough to come into contact with some of these latter twentieth century developments, it would have been interesting to see if his thoughts on *The Family Rite* would have developed further in these directions. Even so, the unpolished thoughts contained in *The Family Rite* deserve attention for the way in which they extend his more considered views elsewhere in his writings and foreshadow, even if in a glass darkly, developments in church and mission that were just around the corner.

# BIBLIOGRAPHY

## BOOKS BY ROLAND ALLEN
## (IN CHRONOLOGICAL ORDER)

Allen, Roland. *The Siege of the Peking Legations.* London: Smith, Elder, 1901.

———. *Foundation Principles of Foreign Missions.* Suffolk: Richard Clay and Sons, 1910.

———. *Missionary Methods: St. Paul's or Ours?* London: Robert Scott, 1912. Reprinted, London: World Dominion Press, 1930, 1949, 1956; Grand Rapids, MI: William B. Eerdmans, 1962, 1998.

———. *Missionary Principles.* London: Robert Scott, 1913. Reprinted as *Essential Missionary Principles.* New York: Fleming H. Revell Company, 1913.

———. *Pentecost and the World: The Revelation of the Holy Spirit in "The Acts of the Apostles."* London: Oxford University Press, 1917.

———. *Educational Principles and Missionary Methods: The Application of Educational Principles to Missionary Evangelism.* London: Robert Scott, 1919.

———. *Voluntary Clergy.* London: S.P.C.K., 1923.

———. *The Spontaneous Expansion of the Church and the Causes which Hinder It.* London: World Dominion Press, 1927. Re-issued, 1949 and 1956. London: World Dominion Press, 1960.

———. *Voluntary Clergy Overseas: An Answer to the Fifth World Call.* Beaconsfield: privately printed, 1928.

———. *Sidney James Wells Clark: A Vision of Foreign Missions.* London: World Dominion Press, 1937.

———. *The Case for Voluntary Clergy.* London: Eyre and Spottiswoode, 1940.

———. *The Ministry of the Spirit: Selected Writings of Roland Allen*, edited by David M. Paton. Grand Rapids, MI: William B. Eerdmans Publishing Company, 1960.

———. *Reform of the Ministry: A Study in the Work of Roland Allen*, edited by David M. Paton. London: Lutterworth Press, 1968.

———. *The Compulsion of the Spirit: A Roland Allen Reader*, edited by David Paton and Charles H. Long. Grand Rapids, MI: William B. Eerdmans; Cincinnati, OH: Forward Movement Publications, 1983.

Allen, Roland and Thomas Cochrane. *Missionary Survey as an Aid to Intelligent Co-operation in Foreign Missions.* London: Longmans, Green, 1920.

## PAMPHLETS BY ROLAND ALLEN (IN CHRONOLOGICAL ORDER)

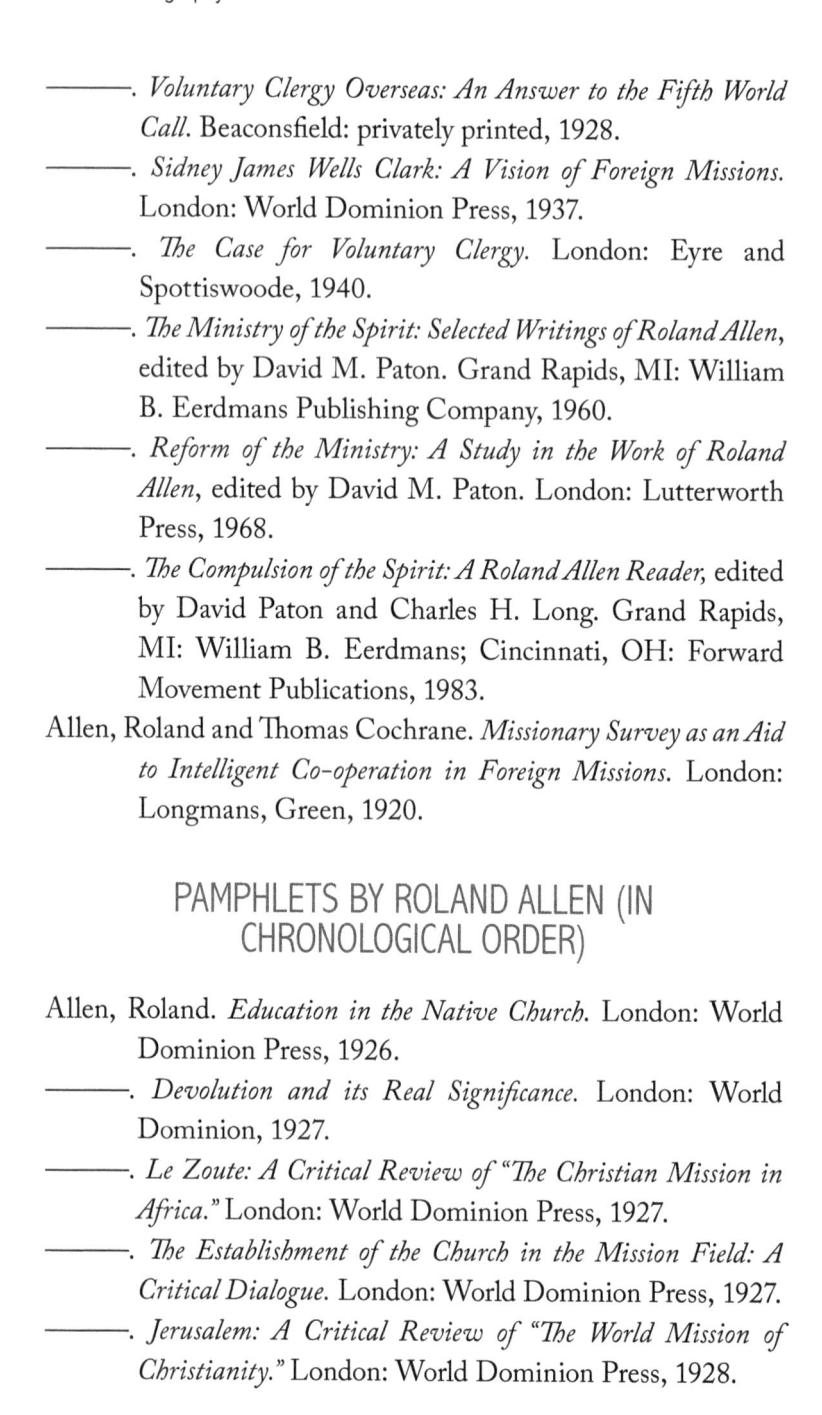

Allen, Roland. *Education in the Native Church.* London: World Dominion Press, 1926.

———. *Devolution and its Real Significance.* London: World Dominion, 1927.

———. *Le Zoute: A Critical Review of "The Christian Mission in Africa."* London: World Dominion Press, 1927.

———. *The Establishment of the Church in the Mission Field: A Critical Dialogue.* London: World Dominion Press, 1927.

———. *Jerusalem: A Critical Review of "The World Mission of Christianity."* London: World Dominion Press, 1928.

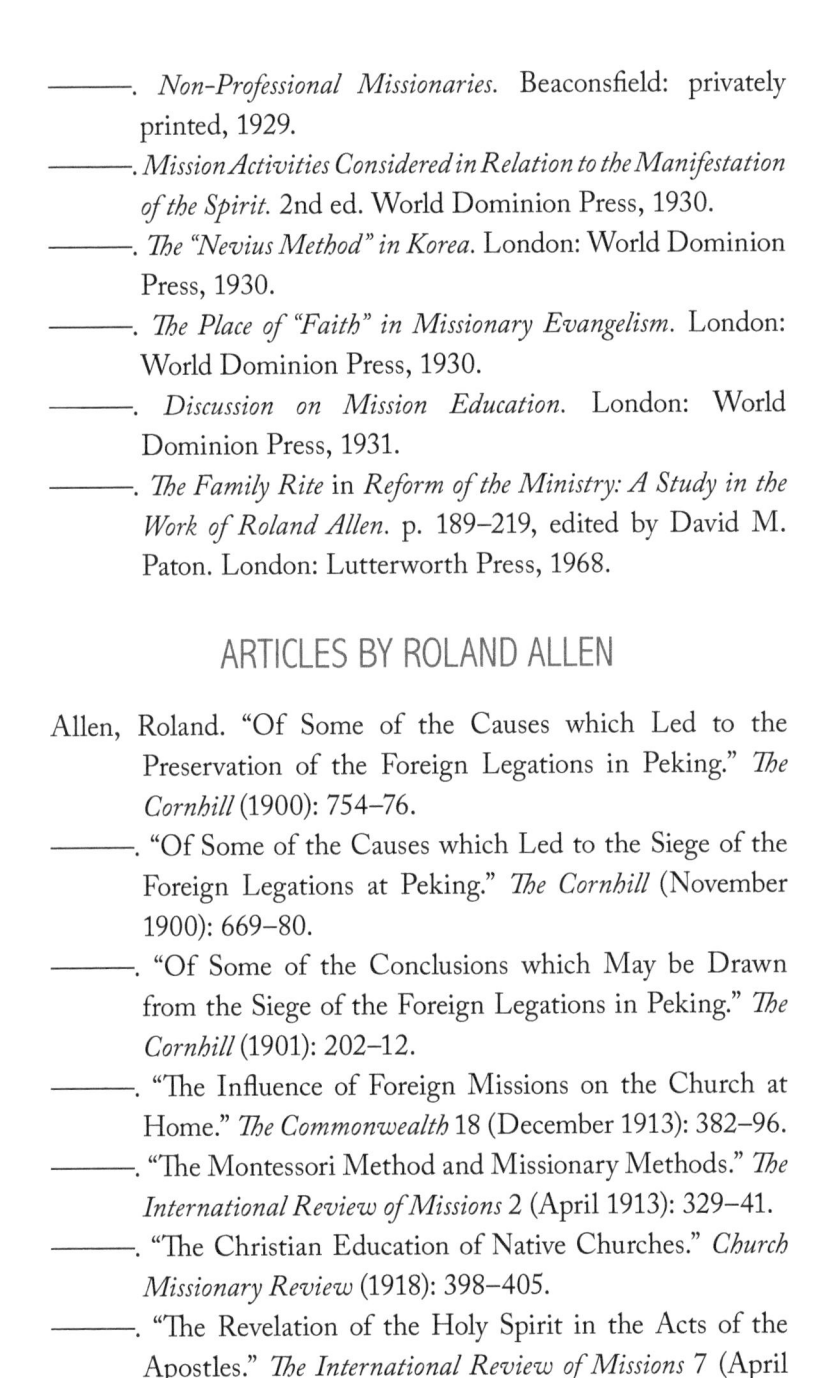

———. *Non-Professional Missionaries*. Beaconsfield: privately printed, 1929.
———. *Mission Activities Considered in Relation to the Manifestation of the Spirit*. 2nd ed. World Dominion Press, 1930.
———. *The "Nevius Method" in Korea*. London: World Dominion Press, 1930.
———. *The Place of "Faith" in Missionary Evangelism*. London: World Dominion Press, 1930.
———. *Discussion on Mission Education*. London: World Dominion Press, 1931.
———. *The Family Rite* in *Reform of the Ministry: A Study in the Work of Roland Allen*. p. 189–219, edited by David M. Paton. London: Lutterworth Press, 1968.

## ARTICLES BY ROLAND ALLEN

Allen, Roland. "Of Some of the Causes which Led to the Preservation of the Foreign Legations in Peking." *The Cornhill* (1900): 754–76.
———. "Of Some of the Causes which Led to the Siege of the Foreign Legations at Peking." *The Cornhill* (November 1900): 669–80.
———. "Of Some of the Conclusions which May be Drawn from the Siege of the Foreign Legations in Peking." *The Cornhill* (1901): 202–12.
———. "The Influence of Foreign Missions on the Church at Home." *The Commonwealth* 18 (December 1913): 382–96.
———. "The Montessori Method and Missionary Methods." *The International Review of Missions* 2 (April 1913): 329–41.
———. "The Christian Education of Native Churches." *Church Missionary Review* (1918): 398–405.
———. "The Revelation of the Holy Spirit in the Acts of the Apostles." *The International Review of Missions* 7 (April 1918): 160–67.

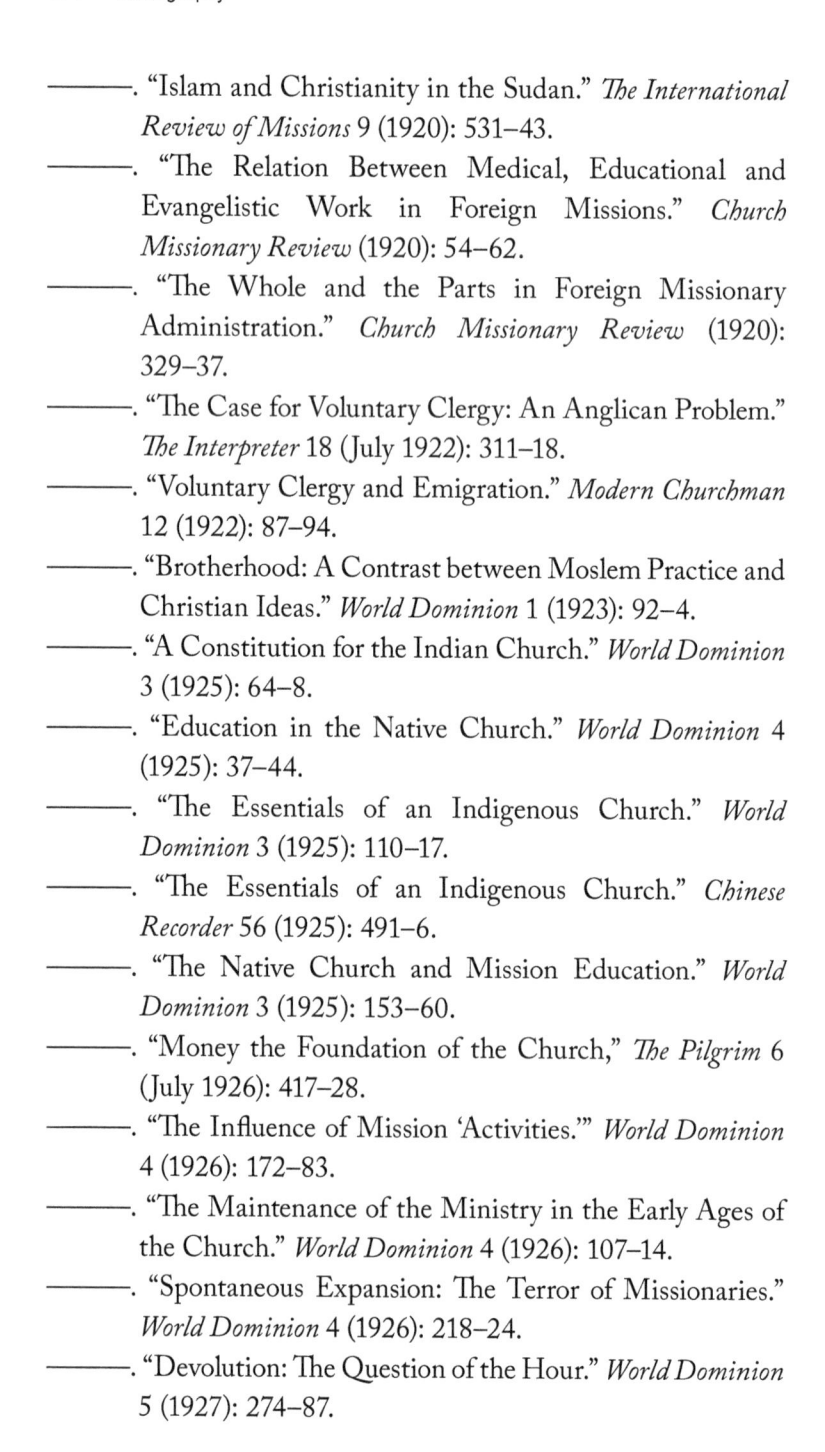

---. "Islam and Christianity in the Sudan." *The International Review of Missions* 9 (1920): 531–43.

---. "The Relation Between Medical, Educational and Evangelistic Work in Foreign Missions." *Church Missionary Review* (1920): 54–62.

---. "The Whole and the Parts in Foreign Missionary Administration." *Church Missionary Review* (1920): 329–37.

---. "The Case for Voluntary Clergy: An Anglican Problem." *The Interpreter* 18 (July 1922): 311–18.

---. "Voluntary Clergy and Emigration." *Modern Churchman* 12 (1922): 87–94.

---. "Brotherhood: A Contrast between Moslem Practice and Christian Ideas." *World Dominion* 1 (1923): 92–4.

---. "A Constitution for the Indian Church." *World Dominion* 3 (1925): 64–8.

---. "Education in the Native Church." *World Dominion* 4 (1925): 37–44.

---. "The Essentials of an Indigenous Church." *World Dominion* 3 (1925): 110–17.

---. "The Essentials of an Indigenous Church." *Chinese Recorder* 56 (1925): 491–6.

---. "The Native Church and Mission Education." *World Dominion* 3 (1925): 153–60.

---. "Money the Foundation of the Church," *The Pilgrim* 6 (July 1926): 417–28.

---. "The Influence of Mission 'Activities.'" *World Dominion* 4 (1926): 172–83.

---. "The Maintenance of the Ministry in the Early Ages of the Church." *World Dominion* 4 (1926): 107–14.

---. "Spontaneous Expansion: The Terror of Missionaries." *World Dominion* 4 (1926): 218–24.

---. "Devolution: The Question of the Hour." *World Dominion* 5 (1927): 274–87.

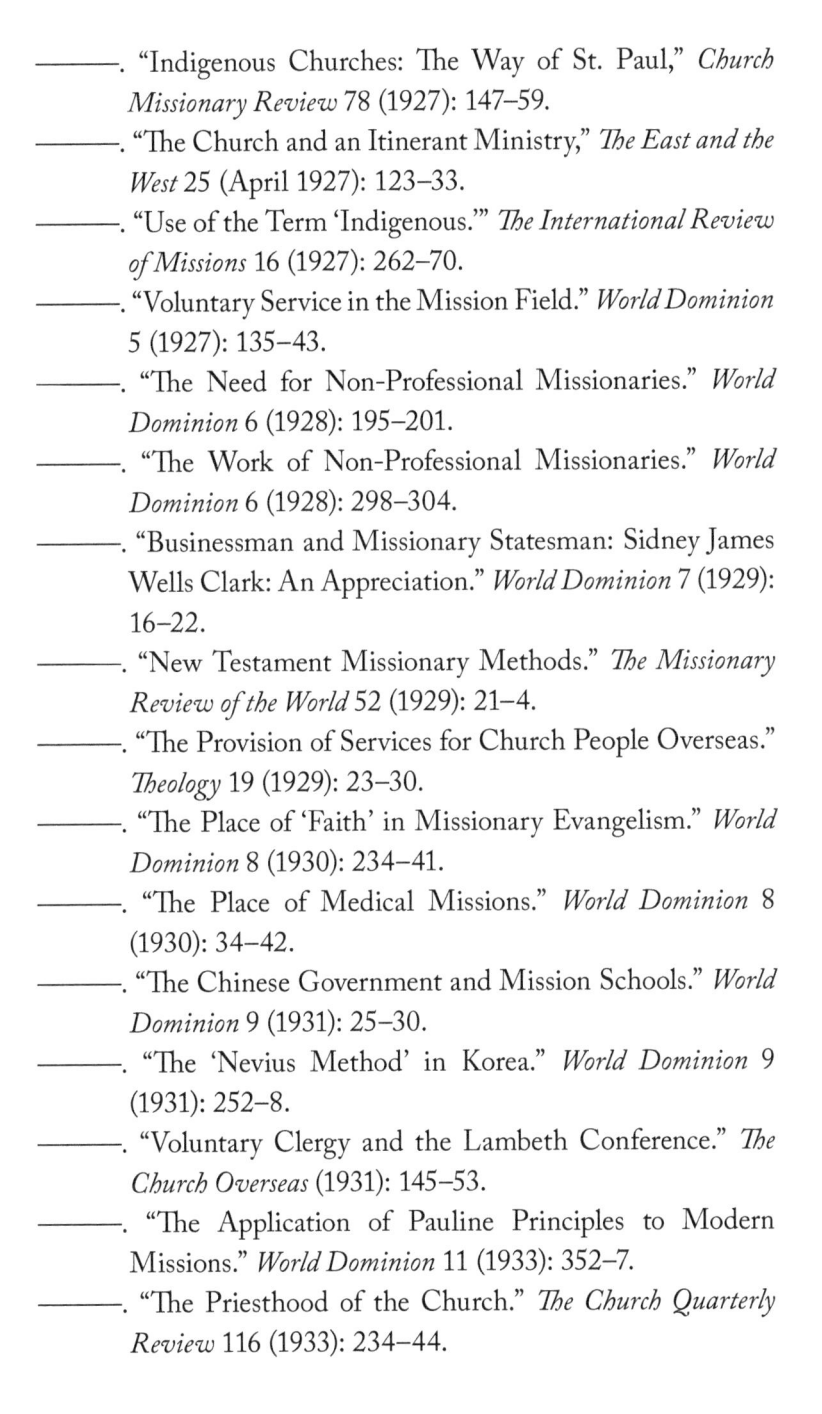

———. "Indigenous Churches: The Way of St. Paul," *Church Missionary Review* 78 (1927): 147–59.

———. "The Church and an Itinerant Ministry," *The East and the West* 25 (April 1927): 123–33.

———. "Use of the Term 'Indigenous.'" *The International Review of Missions* 16 (1927): 262–70.

———. "Voluntary Service in the Mission Field." *World Dominion* 5 (1927): 135–43.

———. "The Need for Non-Professional Missionaries." *World Dominion* 6 (1928): 195–201.

———. "The Work of Non-Professional Missionaries." *World Dominion* 6 (1928): 298–304.

———. "Businessman and Missionary Statesman: Sidney James Wells Clark: An Appreciation." *World Dominion* 7 (1929): 16–22.

———. "New Testament Missionary Methods." *The Missionary Review of the World* 52 (1929): 21–4.

———. "The Provision of Services for Church People Overseas." *Theology* 19 (1929): 23–30.

———. "The Place of 'Faith' in Missionary Evangelism." *World Dominion* 8 (1930): 234–41.

———. "The Place of Medical Missions." *World Dominion* 8 (1930): 34–42.

———. "The Chinese Government and Mission Schools." *World Dominion* 9 (1931): 25–30.

———. "The 'Nevius Method' in Korea." *World Dominion* 9 (1931): 252–8.

———. "Voluntary Clergy and the Lambeth Conference." *The Church Overseas* (1931): 145–53.

———. "The Application of Pauline Principles to Modern Missions." *World Dominion* 11 (1933): 352–7.

———. "The Priesthood of the Church." *The Church Quarterly Review* 116 (1933): 234–44.

## BOOKS ABOUT ROLAND ALLEN

Allen, Hubert J. B. *Roland Allen: Pioneer, Priest, and Prophet.* Cincinnati, OH: Forward Movement Publications; Grand Rapids, MI: William B. Eerdmans, 1995.

Payne, J. D. *Roland Allen: Pioneer of Spontaneous Expansion.* N.p.: CreateSpace, 2012.

Rutt, Steven. *Roland Allen: A Missionary Life.* United Kingdom: The Lutterworth Press, forthcoming 2018.

———. *Roland Allen: A Theology of Mission.* United Kingdom: The Lutterworth Press, forthcoming 2018.

Milton Keynes UK
Ingram Content Group UK Ltd.
UKHW021948230224
438363UK00009B/969

9 780878 083008